SCHOLASTIC

Easy Ways to
Reach & Teach
English
Language
Learners

Valerie SchifferDanoff

New York • Toronto • London • Auckland • Sydney
Mexico City • New Delhi • Hong Kong • Buenos Aires

Teaching
Resources

Dedication

In language learning there is a tandem exchange. A tandem is designed for two people to move forward at the same time. A tandem exchange is when two people agree to share and learn each other's culture and language—the "I help you to learn and you help me to learn," approach.

Marisa D'Angelis and I learned and moved forward together. The classroom was a space through which our exchange flew freely and still does. I dedicate this book to Marisa and all that we share and learn together.

Acknowledgments

I'd like to acknowledge the following people:

Joan Kazer for being a lifelong friend, great listener and the best adviser. She enriched my understanding of linguistics and speech and language on many a run.

Nanci Colangelo, my ESL colleague and friend, for being there, always.

Donna Furphy for her clear and thoughtful speaking points and for speaking to the point.

Dr. Lawrence Krute of Manhattanville College for providing the inspiring theory behind my practices and his repeated advice, "Don't assume anything" and "More is always better."

Judith Hausman of Manhattanville College and Long Island University for infusing some ESL method into the right places of my practices.

Lauren Cutler and Jennifer Basile-Montenegro for sharing their classrooms with me.

The entire faculty and staff at Mount Kisco Elementary School whose work each day contributes to the success of all our students.

The children I teach and especially those who appear in the pages of this book.

Phyllis Stone and her daughter Sarah Davis for animating the seals and flamingoes.

And Joanna Breeding for replacing extra words with beautiful language.

Copyedited by David Klein

Cover design by Brian LaRossa
Interior design by Kelli Thompson
ISBN-13 978-0-439-90015-7
ISBN-10 0-439-90015-8

1 2 3 4 5 6 7 8 9 10   40   15 14 13 12 11 10 09 08

Contents

Introduction

As a child, growing up in a home where more than one language was spoken, I often wondered why my parents conversed with my sisters and me only in English. On my paternal side I was a first-generation American. My father, who spoke three languages—Hungarian, Yiddish, and English—always spoke to his relatives in Hungarian. So whenever there was a paternal family gathering or family phone call, Hungarian is what I heard.

My mother frequently spoke Yiddish to her relatives and to my father. In fact, Yiddish seemed to be their secret code. When my mother did speak to us in Yiddish it was with some wonderful idiom to express love, anger, or a blessing. Sometimes I meet other people who know these same idioms and we can compare notes about how exactly to say them and what they might mean. But few of us were taught to read or speak Yiddish.

Our parents, having lived through WWII, wanted us to be Americans. Or at least that's what they said. So, despite our rich linguistic heritage, they did not encourage us to learn any language other than English—and I missed out on an opportunity to learn more than one language.

While language experiences at home can be a natural way to learn a second language, most traditional language-learning experiences at school are not. In high school, for example, I had to take a foreign language. My high school class met for only 45 minutes each day. I did not go home and speak Spanish and I had no one with whom to speak Spanish anywhere else. In class, we learned some conversational Spanish, practiced conjugating verbs, and studied Spanish cultural background, but Spanish remained a foreign language to me beyond the spoken and written words. In my adult life I've been able to greet people, address Spanish-speaking parents, and carry on light conversations, but I have never gained the fluency I might have achieved by being immersed in the culture.

Being an Authentic Teacher

Teaching ELLs goes beyond coaching them in the four functions of language: speaking, listening, reading, and writing. Our teaching must also be meaningful and effective. We make that possible as teachers and learners by being aware of what we are doing and why on a daily basis.

That way, our teaching and learning can be "organic," a concept Sylvia Ashton Warner developed and practiced for teaching reading and writing to her Maori her students in New Zealand. I am inspired by her belief that teaching needs to be authentic and celebrate the whole child, their experiences and background, while channeling their knowledge to learn more. The lessons and activities in this book are designed to tap students' interests and keep the learning "real."

Sitting here writing this now, I wish I'd had more of an opportunity to learn another language and more of an affinity for learning it. I wholeheartedly tell my students and their parents how fortunate they are to have the opportunity to speak two languages and how important it is to maintain both languages. This has guided my teaching and writing.

As we better understand the English language learner and the challenges of language acquisition, we have the opportunity to infuse our classrooms with authentic and inviting language experiences for all learners. The pages of this book help you begin that process.

How This Book Is Organized

The first chapter is written to broaden your understanding of English language learners and to raise awareness about the many factors that will impact their ability to learn and acquire English in your classroom. It is followed by a chapter about language learning and language acquisition and begins to build your knowledge of the basic strategies for teaching ELLs at each level of English proficiency. Chapter 3 provides a quick reference for strategies to facilitate an ELL's transition to your class and his or her learning throughout the day.

Chapter 4 is a more comprehensive source for using instructional strategies to support ELLs and has sample lessons for each stage of language acquisition. Chapter 5 covers teaching ELLs through a balanced literacy approach to address their developing language needs. Chapter 6 helps you weave language-development strategies into your content-area teaching, while Chapter 7 discusses how the writing process can benefit ELLs and provides model lessons on teaching writing.

Finally, Chapter 8 covers team teaching, an important part of teaching ELLs. Working with another professional who is an expert in teaching English to Speakers of Other Languages (ESOL) is a rewarding experience that can broaden your knowledge and understanding of English language learners and invigorate your professional growth. If you need a quick reference for a language-learning term I've included in these chapters, check the glossary.

As you begin to read the pages of this book consider the following quotes from *Teacher* by Sylvia Ashton Warner (Simon & Schuster, 1986), which has inspired my teaching.

"What a dangerous activity reading is; teaching is. All this plastering on of foreign stuff. Why plaster on at all when there is so much inside already? If only I could get it out and use it as working material . . .

. . . An organic design. A growing living changing design. The normal healthful design. Unsentimental and merciless and shockingly beautiful."

Chapter 1

UNDERSTANDING THE ENGLISH
LANGUAGE LEARNER (ELL)

Like all learners, each English language learner is different. Each child brings his or her own individual experiences when he or she reaches your classroom. You, the teacher, bring all of your life experiences as well, to educate, differentiate, modify, and communicate to the best of your ability. Knowing and understanding your students can guide your teaching so it is as relevant as it can be to them.

What are some factors in the lives of English language learners that can guide strategies for teaching these students?

■ **Stage of language acquisition or level of proficiency**
How much English does the child know? Does he understand little or no English or is he able to speak and understand most conversational English? Does the child have social language skills such as the ability to ask and respond to simple questions? Knowing the level of a child's proficiency in English is vital for your curriculum. Much language is learned on the playground, during recess. Play is somewhat universal and necessitates it own social language, which often carries over into classroom situations. Of course, acquiring this basic social language is the first step toward acculturating into a new school environment.

Acculturation is the process of adjusting to a second culture and language. It is best for the ELL to maintain his or her first language and culture while acculturating to a new country.

Some ELLs have studied English in their home countries and have achieved some level of proficiency. Keep in mind that English is often taught in other countries in a rigid skill-and-drill style. Grammar and verb tenses are spoken, copied and drilled, with very little opportunity for students to experience spoken conversational English. Yet, knowing some English provides a student with a foothold in the language—for example, these students may be able to read English text, albeit at a lower grade level than their English-only (EO) classmates.

■ **Country of origin and culture**
Knowing a child's country of origin may help you make connections with your ELL students. You can include their cultural origins in lessons, and perhaps when studying folktales, bring in one from that child's country. Studying different cultures enriches your instruction and makes learning more relevant and motivating to everyone.

Reasons for leaving their native country

Reasons for leaving a country can determine whether or not an ELL will have a feeling of permanence in his or her new environment. For example, families from a war-torn country are less likely to return there, while families who have a farm in their native land are more likely to go back, even repeatedly.

Children who have been adopted from another culture into an EO family may assimilate into their new culture, losing much of their own culture. Keep in mind that they are experiencing the new culture at school and at home.

Expectations for returning

Some families come to the United States with a firm plan to return to live in their home countries. Other families do not plan to return. These expectations present different challenges for educators. Some children may leave school for months at a time. They "visit" their native country and then return, having missed much curriculum.

It may help to prepare a packet of work, pencils, crayons, and some books for your student to travel with and keep up on English language development.

Age

Each age provides its own challenges as well as advantages. A kindergarten classroom is very hands-on. ELL students at this age are developing language skills and vocabulary along with their peers and may be able to close the gap more quickly to perform on or near grade level. A fourth-grade classroom is less hands on, and the students' language skills are more sophisticated. On the other hand, older children often have more literacy experiences and more knowledge of academic subjects to tap into as they learn in English.

Native language literacy

It is important to know whether a child can read and write in his or her first language, because these skills can be transferred to a second language. Understanding that letters make words and that words make sentences, the ability to track words on a page, and most importantly, understanding that written words carry meaning, are skills and strategies used in every language.

If a child has native language literacy, a strategy might be to provide books (or even a textbook) in the child's first language to keep the child from falling behind as he or she is learning English.

Length of time in this country, city, school

The amount of time a family has been in the community often determines whether you'll be able to access information that has been kept on a particular child. When files do exist it is sometimes difficult to acquire them even from a neighboring district. The ESOL teacher or school social worker may need to make a formal request. Seeing a previous report card or a family history can be very informative in determining an educational plan for a child.

■ Family life

The more you know about a student's family life—whether the student is EO or an ELL—the better you can help the ELL with issues that arise. For example, does the child act as an interpreter for his or her parents? Is there an older sibling who can help with homework?

■ Motivation

Being motivated to learn is frequently determined by the financial and social needs of the family, the child's age and personality, and peer pressure. A young child is very motivated to communicate on the playground, in the housekeeping corner, or at a birthday party, which is one reason why social language emerges earliest. An older child, especially a teenager, has different needs but also wants to fit in.

If a child's family doesn't expect to be in a country for a long time, he or she might lack motivation to learn the academic language needed to pursue an education. Understanding the learner's motivation can help you provide a combination of materials that are most relevant to the student.

■ Personality

Personality traits are so important that we often spend weeks studying them as a literacy unit. It takes courage to come to a new country and learn all there is to learn. In the same way that learning to read requires a child to be somewhat of a risk taker, so does experimenting with a new language. Some children are such perfectionists that at first they will not even attempt to speak; they may have long silent periods before they begin experimenting with a new language. Someone who is more outgoing is more likely to acculturate faster than a shy child. A calm, persevering personality may be more capable of working on the repeated phrasing needed to learn a new language or to achieve at a higher faster pace. Being aware of these traits or subtle differences can help you work more successfully with your ELLs.

CASE IN POINT:
Different Personalities—Different Learning Experiences

I taught twins who qualified for ESOL services in second and third grade. By their third-grade year, their reading and writing skills began to show a wider range and their personalities began to present themselves during our work sessions more distinctly. One was more distractible than the other and had trouble staying focused while the other sought teacher approval and could clearly persevere to repeat a lesson or make changes in writing or reread. The twin who enjoyed positive teacher feedback and attention excelled and met grade level expectations before her sister, who needed additional help to reach the same goal. Their personalities clearly played a part in their academic success.

What kinds of family background information can further your understanding of an English language learner?

■ **Country of origin and time in the U.S.**

The educational system varies from country to country. Countries like Jamaica and India may teach in English, but their rote teaching methods vary significantly from the style of teaching in the United States.

■ **Family literacy**

A child from a literate family is more likely to have positive reading experiences at home and family members to help with homework and instill the value of education. Children whose families do not read or do not value reading might be especially challenging to reach. The classroom teacher and ESOL teacher can encourage ELL family members to read to children in their native language and attend literacy and adult ESOL classes, which are often held in the evening and may provide babysitting services.

■ **Value placed on education**

In some cultures the education of girls is not valued. The tradition is for the girl to marry, have a family, and take care of the home, and the family throws its support behind the education of its male children.

If an education is not a high priority in a given family this attitude may also affect the timely completion of homework. These conditions may create more of a challenge for you as you work toward helping the student to learn English.

■ **Siblings in school**

Children with older siblings tend to know more English and even achieve at a higher rate. Older siblings often serve as models for speaking English and can help with homework.

■ **Place of birth**

Though many ELLs are foreign-born, some are not. Heritage ELLs were born in this country to parents who speak only their native language at home. Very often these children, like their peers born in other countries, have not attended school until entering kindergarten, so when they arrive at school, they have had few, if any, English language experiences. For some ELLs the only time they speak and hear English is in the school environment.

■ **Home situation**

ELL children often serve as their parents' interpreter because their parents only speak their native language. Once these children start school, they frequently speak English only or a combination of English and their first language. Often these children maintain their receptive vocabulary in order to understand the home language but lose much of their oral language fluency in their native language, and so, answer in English. It is best when children maintain their native language and have parents who can read to them in that language as well.

Knowing the languages spoken at home can be important to home-school connections too. Some schools have translators available and provide translations of important school communications. Keeping parents informed is often critical to helping students acculturate and succeed.

Reasons for leaving native country

Many children and their families have fled their countries because of war and terrorism. So be prepared, careful, gentle, and understanding when inquiring about or discussing family issues. Parents and children can become tearful about their experiences in their native countries even through a translator. Leaving due to traumatic events can have an adverse effect on the time it takes for a child to learn English and adjust to their new school.

Learn About Your Students

Gathering as much background information as possible will help you determine where to begin teaching a particular child.

Cultural differences

In all cultures there are certain things that you may not do or say. For example, in some cultures, eye contact, and therefore, looking the teacher in the eye, is disrespectful. Yet, in American schools the opposite is true. Standing in front of a class and giving the correct answer can be considered showing off in some cultures, while it may be considered being attentive here. Some of the best advice I got while studying for my ESOL certification was, "Don't assume anything."

That's why I recommend going online and learning about a particular culture. Try www.wwcd.org for some general do's and don'ts. A little research before meeting your ELL student can go a long way. Also, check with your school's ESOL teacher, who may have a wealth of knowledge to share as well.

Expectations

In American culture, the expectation for many of us is that our children will graduate from public school and then go to college. Parents help and encourage their children to reach this goal by helping with homework, coming to parent-teacher conferences, and (at least at the elementary level) being somewhat involved and vested in their children's education.

Parents who come from a different culture may not be literate. They may work two, even three, jobs. Or perhaps they began having children at an early age. Their experiences may be different in many ways and so are their expectations and involvement. They are acculturating, too.

Respect for the teacher

As you would expect from parents of EO students, you'll have a range of responses from the parents of your ELLs. In general, many will see you as a key to their child's success and will offer you a great deal of respect and appreciation for the way you teach. Build these relationships whenever you can; when parents offer their respect, gratitude, and support, it has a positive impact on the students and on the home-school connection.

Working closely with English language learners has enriched my teaching experiences and greatly broadened my appreciation and understanding of cultural differences. I have a heightened awareness of language and of the need to communicate using all available resources. I find myself using everything I've learned since kindergarten, and then some, to teach in as meaningful and authentic a way as possible. Taking time to meet individually with your ELLs is part of your learning as a teacher. The more information you can gather and trust you can build, the more successful your instruction will be. The following chapters help you determine and understand your ELLs' language development and address their needs more precisely.

Chapter 2

THE PROCESS OF LANGUAGE ACQUISITION AND LEVELS OF PROFICIENCY

The natural process of language acquisition is defined in different ways by various agencies, authors, and programs. Becoming familiar with the language your district uses to name levels of proficiency for ELLs and then understanding the characteristics of each level, provides you and your colleagues with a common vocabulary to use when discussing and learning about students. This knowledge also gives you a better understanding of how each ELL will progress. In New York State, for example, an ELL is categorized as either a beginner, intermediate, or advanced student based on his or her score on a particular assessment. Each year, ELLs take the New York State English as a Second Language Test, and based on their test score, a student either continues in the program or he or she is identified as proficient in English and ready for mainstream classes without ESOL instructional support.

As you learn where your specific students are in this process, it is also important to keep in mind that the factors described in Chapter 1 will impact the child's progress and motivation to learn. Strategies for reaching and motivating learners at each level follow each of the stages below. (Each level can be further subdivided into low, middle, and high levels of proficiency. However, we generally include these only at the beginner level, where the characteristics among these sublevels are the most discernible and easy to target for instruction.)

Low-Beginner

This level is also referred to as *pre-production, newcomer,* or *silent period.*

The low-beginner ELL is still adjusting to his or her new environment. Everything is new and different. At first he or she may feel elated about the change, but then difficulties in communicating may become overwhelming. It looks as if everyone around the child is having fun and it's frustrating not to be able to participate. This frustration can cause some acting-out behaviors like running out of the room, crying, or even hiding under a table.

It is important to make every effort to speak in a soft, gentle, reassuring voice, but when a child's behavior is unacceptable, taking on a stern tone or look may be the best way to let the ELL know that the behavior is unacceptable. Try to use this voice sparingly, otherwise, as with all children, feelings will be hurt and the point will be lost. This stage usually lasts between three and eight months.

At this early stage, whatever the ELL hears is becoming part of what will be his or her new language. Yet, the child will not understand new words and phrases until they have been repeated many times and in different contexts. In general, a beginner ELL:

- Maintains a silent period

- Relies on visuals

- Responds nonverbally by shaking his/her head

- Depends on gestures and facial expressions, and the use of visuals and manipulatives

- Understands one or two words

- Relies on a translator to be understood

- Writes patterns or words modeled by the teacher

- Begins to repeat language modeled by another person. (Some children will be completely silent.)

- Responds to and follows simple directions, such as "put on your coat"

STRATEGIES FOR THE TEACHER

Using visual cues and gestures to communicate and introducing the school and classroom language in the form of rules, classroom materials, and routines are key. These strategies are detailed in the reading and writing strategies in Chapter 3 and in the Beginner level section in Chapter 4. Having other students act as buddies to the new student is also very helpful in ensuring a safe social environment.

Pictorial representation of classroom math language

ESOL Support Options

When a child has been evaluated and qualifies for ESOL services, he or she may receive different types of assistance from a certified ESOL teacher, including **push-in support**, in which the ESOL teacher works within the classroom, on the class assignment, usually with individual students or in a small decentralized group. Another model is **pull-out support**, in which the ELL spends time learning in an individual or small-group setting outside of the classroom. The ESOL teacher creates lessons that target the stage of the students' language development. A more intensive program is **sheltered instruction**, a separate class in which ELLs do not compete with EOs for instruction. These are most commonly found at a secondary level for teaching content areas.

In all delivery models the ESOL teacher uses physical activities, visual aids, linguistic modifications, and other methods to teach. Be familiar with the types of support your school offers and establish open lines of communication with the ESOL teacher. For ways to develop an effective teaching partnership with the ESOL teacher, see Chapter 8.

Mid-Beginner

This level is also referred to as *early production*.

The mid-beginner ELL has made some adjustments to his or her new environment, and expectations for learning and understanding begin to increase. The ELL continues to experience frustration at not being able to communicate or keep up with his or her peers. At this stage, which may last from two to four months or even longer, the ELL:

- Begins to acquire and use basic social language, may have acquired 500 or more words
- Begins to respond with a couple of words and even short phrases
- Increases receptive vocabulary
- Can comprehend more input
- Continues to use nonverbal gestures
- May be able to write short phrases

Cooperative learning makes learning more meaningful for all students.

STRATEGIES FOR THE TEACHER

Continue to use any low-beginner strategies that have worked well for the student, and offer word choices when posing questions. For example, say, "Would you like a hamburger or pizza for lunch?"; "Do you want to draw with crayons or pencils?"; or "In the story, did the girl eat an orange or an apple?" Also, ask simple questions using words like *who*, *what*, and *where* which lend themselves to one- or two-word responses. A strategy that's especially useful at this stage is Total Physical Response (TPR) and is described in Chapter 4 (pages 34–37). Finally, provide opportunities for ELLs to participate in partner and cooperative learning to encourage language learning with their peers in a meaningful context.

High-Beginner

This level is synonymous with *low intermediate*.

In this stage, which may last one to two years, the ELL is more comfortable in the classroom setting and in expressing his wants and needs, and showing more interest in learning. A student's social language may be fairly well developed—to the point where it can be deceptive. You may think the student's oral, social language is good enough to expect more from him or her academically. However, the student's academic language has yet to develop. An ELL at this stage:

- Continues to be unresponsive at times

- Continues to increase his or her receptive vocabulary

- Has acquired about 1,500 to 2,000 words and can use them in oral language

- Speaks to meet basic needs. The ELL can ask to go to the bathroom, get a drink of water, or go to the nurse and tell you he or she needs more of an explanation.

- Responds in short phrases rather than with one word. For example, "I want pizza for lunch."

- Speaks in phrases that may not be grammatically correct all of the time. Note that correct usage of pronouns and prepositions develops more slowly than other language skills. You might hear, for example, "I sit over to Josh." Or "This is mines pencil."

- Experiments with language and seeks the correct usage. For example:

Student: I like to red color my picture.

Teacher: You want to use the red crayon for your picture?

Student: Yes, I want the red crayon for my picture.

- Begins to read and write some low-level text that is contextualized and pictorially supported

- Understands some basic information in context. When listening to a picture book about food, the ELL has acquired enough vocabulary to respond to questions about it.

STRATEGIES FOR THE TEACHER

In addition to any low- and mid-beginner strategies that are working, also begin to provide graphic organizers and sentence starters that can help the ELL understand basic information and improve his or her writing. For instance, a pictorial sequencing activity can be very helpful for retelling a story. Also, the teacher can model language to encourage a discussion. For example:

Student: I like eat pizza.

Teacher: I like to eat pizza with my friends.

Student: I like to eat pizza with my friends.

Teacher: I like to eat pizza with my family, too.

Student: I eat pizza with my mama.

Teacher: I like my pizza with lots of cheese.

Student: I like lots of cheese with pizza.

An ELL with a more outgoing personality or with native-language literacy may pass through the above stages more quickly. A student with an outgoing personality has the confidence that may allow him or her to experiment more with language and not worry about making mistakes. An ELL who does not have a peer group with whom he or she can speak his or her first language may also pass through these stages more quickly.

Intermediate

This level is also referred to as *intermediate fluency.*

The ELL is gaining proficiency in both social and academic language, and is becoming much more involved in his or her own learning. This stage can last two to four years before peer-level proficiencies develop. At this stage, an ELL:

- Understands more conversation and dialogue

- Can tell or retell a simple story

- Asks questions for a purpose, such as, "How do you play this game?" Or "Can I play that game next?" as opposed to academic questions, which develop later in this and the next stage, such as, "What is the Civil War?" or "Why did people fight this war?"

- Continues to experiment with vocabulary and grammar both verbal and written

CASE IN POINT:
Who's More Advanced?

Alejandro and Esteban were third graders who shared a similar cultural background but had very different educational experiences.

Alejandro was educated through the second grade and had excellent literacy skills in his native language. Despite his first language literacy, Alejandro was not progressing as quickly as expected. His teacher gave him a Spanish version of the math textbook so he could keep up in that subject area. Additionally, he was pulled out every day for 90 minutes into a newcomer group to develop vocabulary and received push-in support for 70 minutes a day as part of the class group.

Esteban came to the U.S. a year before Alejandro arrived, with no school experience. He could speak conversationally, with very little discernible accent, while Alejandro, after six months, could not. Though Esteban often acted as a translator for Alejandro, he struggled all year to develop literacy skills. By the end of the year Esteban had begun to acquire a sight word vocabulary and was beginning to read and apply some phonics skills for decoding but inconsistently.

Speaking to Esteban, one might have thought that he did not need ESOL support because he expressed himself so well in English. But while his social language (BICS) was so strong, Esteban's grasp of academic language (CALP) was very weak. He would need much more time to develop literacy skills in English, as well as time to gain the academic vocabulary that he had not acquired in his first language. On the other hand, Alejandro's first-language literacy skills enhanced his second-language learning, enabling him to catch up more to his peers academically.

Bottom line: do not be fooled by how well a child speaks. He or she may still need a lot of academic language support to read and write within grade level expectations.

- Takes some risks with word choices, verbal and written

- Still makes grammar or vocabulary mistakes

- Requires patience from teachers and peers when speaking

- Sometimes gives up if he or she is misunderstood or asked to repeat a verbal response too many times

- Writes more independently

STRATEGIES FOR THE TEACHER

Ask ELLs questions that require some extended thought processes, like, "What do you do when . . . ?" or "How do you . . . ?" Make sure to provide opportunities for describing, comparing, retelling, and defining, and encourage the student to describe to another student how to do something. Conversely, teach questioning skills in the context of content-area learning, an approach described in Chapter 4 (pages 37–39).

Advanced

Some ELLs will move more quickly than others from the intermediate to the advanced stage of language acquisition. Once the transition has begun you may see subtle or rapid development depending upon a number of factors, including intrinsic motivation, support from peers and family, and other factors mentioned in Chapter 1.

An ELL at this stage has been acquiring his or her new language for about three to five years. The student has an expressive vocabulary of about 3,000 to 4,000 English words and communicates socially with confidence in his or her peer group. This is when reading and writing comprehension in English begins to develop with more momentum. However, the demands for comprehending grade-level texts and actually learning academically in English are still very different from the demands of conversational English.

Social Learning Versus Academic Learning

Even at this stage, when students may sound quite fluent in English, do not be misled by a child's spoken language proficiency. Learning to speak a language is very different from learning in that language. People often speak conversational language for years without ever using that language to learn academic content. All learners typically acquire about 1,000 new words a year. That means an ELL arriving in first grade with no English language has a deficit of 6,000 words compared to their English speaking peers. Keeping that in mind, by grade five an ELL will have acquired about 4,000 English words as compared to the native-language speaker who has acquired a base core vocabulary of 10,000 English words.

At this stage the ELL:

- Speaks more fluently but still makes occasional errors

- Understands and can respond to conversation spoken at natural rate

- Reads and writes one to two years below grade-level expectations

- Writes independently and can work on editing and revising

- May still have difficulty with idiomatic and idiosyncratic language

STRATEGIES FOR THE TEACHER

Keep in mind that your ELL students' cognitive academic language proficiency (CALP) continues to develop at this stage. Provide a variety of texts for your ELLs. Ask questions that require an opinion, prediction, or inference. Be sure to provide students with an idiom dictionary and encourage classmates to explain the meaning of unfamiliar or confusing terms for their peers. Word study strategies for this level will help students stay engaged in language learning (see Chapter 4, pages 40–41 for a word-study lesson idea.)

As an ELL tests out of ESOL services, there is a period of transition before the student is fully proficient. Some educational settings provide various types of support during the transitional stage, including pull-out and push-in options.

While the stages of language acquisition may help us see the challenges our students face and the possibilities for reaching them more clearly, the way each child progresses through the stages is different. From the eager kindergartner, for whom everything is new and exciting, to the quiet third grader who arrives at school with literacy skills and other knowledge in his or her own language to share, there is no typical English language learner. Like all students, ELLs are part of the classroom community. Every day your students are strengthening their ability to learn and communicate—and you are one of their primary resources. Chapter 3 provides basic strategies for classroom set up and instruction that will help you welcome and support your ELLs and the rest of the class.

Chapter 3

STRATEGIES AT A GLANCE

Many language-development strategies used by ESOL teachers are easily adaptable to the general curriculum because they benefit all the students in your classroom and can contribute to differentiated instruction. Much of what the ESOL teacher does is best practice teaching—and you may recognize and already use some of the strategies covered in this chapter. The more you integrate these strategies in your teaching, the more comfortable ELLs will be in your classroom and the more motivated they will be to learn English and the content you teach.

Classroom Setup Strategies

Making your classroom ELL friendly will keep your EO students on track, too. A good classroom setup saves you time by making resources and supplies readily available for you and your students. For example, students can be more responsible for working independently when a map or word wall is right in front of them and easily accessible. Students are more comfortable when asked to write or illustrate when pencils, crayons, and other materials are within reach. A well-planned classroom setup makes the space more inviting and efficient for everyone.

Here are a few pointers:

- When placing tables and desks, think about creating spaces that can be used for various setups: partner work and small or large groups. Can desks be moved aside or grouped easily?

- Follow a daily routine and post your schedule using graphics or a rebus format if possible. When students know what to expect of their day, they are more comfortable. Frequently, one of the first things ELLs learn is the day on which they have a special class like gym or music. All students seem to like knowing what time they have lunch or recess!

Clustering desks encourages partner and small-group work.

- Place responsibility for learning on the students. Keeping supplies, math manipulative materials, and reference books within reach of the students enables them to access what they need on their own.

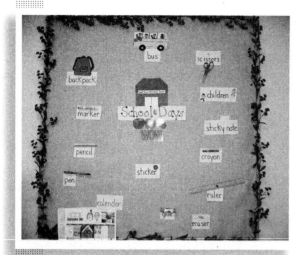

A back-to-school bulletin board using realia

■ Set up your classroom with word walls that have pictures or real objects (realia) connected to them.

■ Display rebus charts to provide pictorial cues along with word cues.

■ Use graphics such as maps, photographs, and other visual displays as much as possible.

■ Have plenty of chart paper on hand for recording strategies, word banks, and other class-generated ideas. Having more than one pad or stand accessible is helpful too. Keep a stand placed where large group instruction occurs and one placed for small-group instruction.

■ Gather materials that can be used for hands-on learning, such as math manipulative materials, sensory learning materials (e.g., sandpaper letters), maps, and graphs.

■ Set up a classroom library that includes a listening center with books on tape and earphones. Children love to listen to a story. ELLs can listen to a book on tape that they are not yet ready to read on their own. I find that my ELLs especially love to listen to song books and you may hear them singing along.

General Instructional Strategies

These strategies are part good thinking and part best practices. They work for ELLs and EO students because they activate prior knowledge, encourage students to work together, and provide sensible foundations for teaching and learning in a classroom setting. They can be realistically integrated into the classroom and provide all learners with opportunities to use the four functions of language in an authentic context. (You'll find most of these strategies described in more detail in Chapter 4.)

■ Never assume anything! What you think a student does or does not know can greatly affect the success of a lesson or activity. For example, some children may not have had experience with cutting or gluing. A quick demonstration can prevent heartache or a big mess.

■ Differentiate instruction and recognize multiple intelligences when designing lessons. Activities should include different kinds of opportunities for individual, paired, and group work, as well as tasks that appeal to a range of learners, like creating charts, drawing, gathering information, and presenting. Differentiating enables your teaching to connect with more of your students.

For more on this subject, check out *Differentiation in Action: A Complete Resource With Research-Supported Strategies to Help You Plan and Organize Differentiated Instruction* by Judith Dodge (Scholastic, 2006) and *Multiple Intelligences: The Theory in Practice* by Howard Gardner (Basic Books, 1993).

- Teach thematically whenever possible so that students have multiple opportunities to use the words they are learning in context. (See Word Bank examples on page 23.)

- Provide choices for completing a project. Guide and evaluate students' work with a rubric. (See Chapter 6.)

- Draw pictures to explain vocabulary. Have a student volunteer draw the pictures, too, and post them in the classroom or have students draw pictures in notebooks or on a chart.

- Repeat the same lesson or concept in different ways; more exposure to new learning is always better.

- Color code and/or number directions posted in your classroom.

- Repeat vocabulary in a variety of ways through reading, writing, listening, and speaking experiences.

- Infuse activities with higher level thinking skills, such as comparing, evaluating, extrapolating, and synthesizing, as in the description of the Character Study lesson in Chapter 5.

A student explains written information using her oral language skills.

Reading and Writing Strategies

These strategies provide opportunities for all students to read, write, listen, and speak in a variety of contexts. They also provide ways for you to organize lessons and student work, and encourage students to be accountable. While most of these strategies are designed for use in a balanced literacy program, you can easily adapt them to meet your specific program needs.

For more about balanced literacy, see Chapter 5 and check out these resources. *How to Reach and Teach All Children Through Balanced Literacy* by Sandra F. Rief and Julie A. Heimburge (Jossey-Bass, 2007), *Reading With Meaning* by Debi Miller (Stenhouse, 2002), and *On Solid Ground: Strategies for Teaching Reading* by Sharon Taberski (Heinemann, 2000).

- For unit studies, gather a variety of books on the same subject, making sure that the books reflect the range of reading levels in your class.

- Teach comprehension first. Skills like phonics can be developed after meaning is established or receptive and expressive vocabulary is strong.

- Plan comprehension-building activities before, during, and after the reading, such as picture walks (looking at and discussing the pictures in a book before reading to build background) and writing a personal response.

- Brainstorm with the whole class to generate a word bank for writing. (See page 23.)

- Teach the strategy of using pictorial, semantic, and syntax cues, and conventions of print to read for meaning.

- Encourage children to predict, confirm, and self correct.

- Generate a list of questions about what you are reading.

- Discuss new words in context. For ELLs, reading experiences are filled with unfamiliar vocabulary that is specific to our culture.

- Teach word-study skills. For example, classifying and sorting words by spelling patterns helps students develop vocabulary and provides opportunities to transfer spelling concepts from reading to writing.

- Integrate reading with writing and use a variety of genres and formats as a springboard for writing activities.

  - Work with recipes. Recipes are a great example of meaningful procedural text. They are a motivating hands-on activity and can serve as models for procedural writing.

  - Have students keep journals for personal narratives and content-area learning. Journals keep students organized and accountable for their work. After a weekend or holiday, rereading what has been recorded in journals lets ELLs review the subject and get back on track. Parents love seeing these too.

- Incorporate environmental print into your classroom with examples from magazines, newspapers, ads, street signs, and other sources.

Speaking Strategies

Being able to speak English fluently is critical to our ELLs' success both inside and outside the classroom. ELLs must pass a speaking portion of a language proficiency assessment to score out of ESOL services and be fully immersed in mainstream classes without support.

We always see a number of students, from every cultural background, who are too shy to speak up in the classroom or to answer a question, even when they have the answer. These strategies help all students improve their language development in a supportive, encouraging way. At the end of the list are some strategies specific to helping ELLs acquire and use oral language.

- Model language by saying aloud and writing the ideas and concepts you're teaching.

- Model what a fluent reader sounds like through focused read-alouds.

- Be explicit. Give each activity you do a name, the simplest and most accurate name that you can, and then repeat the activity, so students can learn the verbal and written cues and procedures.

- Tell students what they are learning about each day and whether they will be reading, writing, listening, or speaking.

- Make expectations clear for behavior, written assignments, independent practice, and group work. Write key expectations on a chart and keep the chart posted for reference. Use a rubric whenever possible to help students evaluate their behavior and work.

The Power of Word Banks

Word Banks—lists of words generated by the class and related to a topic of study—are simple, yet powerful tools. By brainstorming to create the word bank, all students have the opportunity to speak, listen to each other, and experience reading and writing with words related to their learning. Posted as a reference, a word bank encourages students to review past knowledge and use the words listed to integrate content in their writing, as in the following example.

A third-grade class I was working with had just completed a study of different kinds of clouds and precipitation. To integrate their learning with our poetry unit, we asked the class to brainstorm words about spring and spring weather. To get their ideas flowing, we went back and discussed one of the books from their recent science unit—a technique known as touchstoning. Showing the cover and doing a quick picture walk through the book activated the students' prior knowledge, allowing them to revisit what they already knew.

Spring Word Bank				
Weather	Activities	Smells	Sights	Sounds
clouds	baseball	blossoms	rainbows	boom
cirrus	swimming	flowers	butterflies	crash
cumulus	catching insects	rain	green grass	drip-drop
stratus	finding tadpoles	wetness	baby birds	thunder
fog	fishing	sweat	bird's eggs	birds
rain	puddle jumping	apple blossoms	clouds	buzzing
water droplets	playing outside	fresh air	lightning	crack
lightning	swimming	barbecue	lilacs	crash
atmosphere	riding bikes	worms	dandelions	sizzle
clear sky	digging		buds	plip-plop
climate	planting		blossoms	spring peepers
condensation	running		mud	tweet
water vapor			puddles	ah-choo!
contrails			mist	
dew point			worms	
funnel cloud				
overcast				

A brainstorm of spring words

After listing all the science vocabulary associated with clouds and weather, the students naturally progressed to listing other words they associated with spring. The word bank grew to include spring activities, smells, sights, and sounds. We were even able to introduce the poetic element of onomatopoeia when discussing spring sounds like the "boom!" of thunder. The students then wrote their own individual poems, using the word bank as a resource. This type of contextualized repetition helps all students—and especially ELLs—retain content-area vocabulary and use it.

Keeping the word bank available is also helpful for assisting students who needed more individualized instruction or who have been absent. The chart is also a good resource to promote buddy work: Have an EO student review the word bank with a student who is still learning the language.

- Have students retell stories aloud. Record their retellings in their own words to create a language experience chart that can be used for future reading and writing lessons with this group.

- Teach choral speaking and reading (poetry may be the most accessible format with which to begin).

- Sing or read songs. Children can bring in a favorite song to perform alone or as a group, but make sure you have heard the song first and can approve it.

- Have students read and perform Readers Theater scripts.

Check out *Readers Theater for Building Fluency: Strategies and Scripts for Making the Most of This Highly Effective, Motivating, and Research-Based Approach to Oral Reading* by Jo Worthy (Scholastic, 2005).

- Practice dictation, especially for learning spelling. Allow students to take turns dictating, too. Use full sentences for contextualizing the spelling words.

- Experiment with speaking and writing in different tenses and using different types of expressive language. For example, say the same word or phrase using a tone that is happy, sad, angry, and so forth. Use facial expressions—a smile, frown, or quizzical look—to embed more meaning in your speech. For beginners, hold up picture cards showing expressive faces and have them act out these expressions.

- Explain by showing, not just telling. Act it out if you have to or use visual tools such as sketches and diagrams or actual objects.

- Correct content, not grammar. To model proper grammar and syntax, restate or rephrase students' questions or statements. You can do this in writing too.

Student: I put mines pencil on that desk.

Teacher: I put my pencil on that desk, too.

OR

Student: Who go to bring lunch count today?

Teacher: Hmmm, let's see . . . Who is going to bring the lunch count to the office today?

- To express proper intonation and pitch, be aware that you modulate your voice, make adjustments in tone, and use a range of pitch with everything you say to your students. We do this naturally anyway; for example, our voices rise at the end of a question.

- When asking questions, give choices for the answer. This will also help you check for understanding especially in the earlier stages of language acquisition. For example, ask, "Would you like pizza or a bagel for lunch?" Or, after reading a story, ask, "Did the first pig build his house of bricks or straw?"

- Respond to the interests of the children. Provide reading, speaking, listening, and writing activities and opportunities in which students can share their hobbies and interests.

- Encourage students to describe, summarize, define, contrast, and compare by modeling. Be sure to show and not just tell when teaching a new concept, idea, or vocabulary.

- Be your own glossary. If you use an unfamiliar word, define it for the class as part of your lesson.

- Don't assume that students truly understand the subject being discussed just because they are nodding and even answering your questions. Monitor what you say to make sure that they understand. When in doubt, ask the class to restate the directions you've given or the ideas you've presented.

- Ask students to give multiple meanings of a particular word or tell whether it can be labeled a verb or a noun. This will help students sharpen their grammar skills and place ideas in the context of your discussion.

CASE IN POINT:
Assumptions Can Get in the Way

Rosa had been in school for three years and was my student for two years. She was a second grader who spoke English well. We were working to improve her developing reading and academic language skills. Before reading a book about a child getting ready for school in the morning, we did a picture walk and discussed the activity shown on each page in a general way (waking up, getting dressed, eating breakfast, washing her face, brushing her teeth, and combing her hair). I wanted to go over some of the vocabulary in context so that Rosa could work on using phonics cues.

As Rosa was reading, she came to a page on which the text and illustration described several items on a counter, including a towel, soap, comb, toothbrush, and toothpaste. When I pointed to the toothpaste in the picture she was able to say the word *toothpaste*. I assumed (red flag!) that she would recognize the word *toothbrush* when it came up in the next sentence because of its structure, syntax, and context: we had even talked about the girl in the picture brushing her teeth.

She struggled and struggled with the word *toothbrush*, even when I covered up the last part of the word, *brush*. Finally, I pointed to the picture and asked if she used one at home. She replied, "Yes."

"Well what do you call it?"

"I don't know" she replied. "I only know that word in Spanish."

- Develop vocabulary over time, in different learning contexts—use the target words in large and small groups and one-on-one formats. Post vocabulary words in the room on chart paper.

For Beginner ELLs

- Use a minimum of pronouns. State the person, place, or thing you're referring to repeatedly, if necessary. For example, to the question "Does Juan have his book?" you might answer, "No, I think Juan needs to borrow your book," rather than "No, I think he needs to borrow yours.")

- Use limited tenses when speaking to a beginner.

- Use fewer words, pause often, and check your rate of speaking for the newcomer and beginner; you may need to slow down and simplify your speech.

These strategies are designed to enhance, rather than cramp, your style. For instance, using journals may help with organizing your students' work; experimenting with Readers Theater may be another way to teach expressive, fluent reading; brainstorming and using word banks more often will provide your students with additional opportunities for speaking, listening to each other, reading, and writing. And providing more of these language-development opportunities in your instruction supports language growth for every student. The next chapter provides specific strategies and lessons to help you reach ELLs at each level of language development.

Materials That Are Great to Have on Hand

These materials and resources will help you and your ELL students communicate more effectively.

Teacher References

Longman Dictionary of American English (Addison Wesley Longman, 1997)

The New First Dictionary of Cultural Literacy by E.D. Hirsch (Houghton Mifflin, 2004)

Usborne Introduction to Learn Spanish by Nicole Irving (Usborne, 1992)

Picture Dictionaries

The New Oxford Picture Dictionary by E. C. Parnell (Oxford Press, 1989)

Oxford Picture Dictionary for the Content Areas by Dorothy Kauffman and Gary Apple (Oxford University Press, 2000)

Scholastic First Picture Dictionary (Scholastic, 2005)

Bilingual Picture Dictionaries

Hippocrene Children's Illustrated Spanish Dictionary (Hippocrene Books, 2003). Also available in Russian, French, Japanese, Norwegian, Swedish, Arabic, German, Portuguese, Chinese, and Dutch.

The Oxford Picture Dictionary for the Content Areas: English-Spanish Dictionary

My World in Italian Coloring Book and Picture Dictionary by Tamara Mealer (National Text-book Company, 1992)

Usborne Picture Dictionary in Spanish by Felicity Brooks (Usborne, 2003)

Other Great Language Reference Materials

Clear and Simple Thesaurus by Harriet Wittels (Scholastic, 1996)

Scholastic Children's Thesaurus by John Bollard (Scholastic, 1998)

Scholastic Dictionary of Idioms by Marvin Terban (Scholastic, 2006)

Scholastic Dictionary of Synonyms, Antonyms and Homonyms (Scholastic, 2001)

A Child's Picture Dictionary English/ Chinese by Dennis Sheheen (Adana Books, 1987)

"Usborne's Animated First 1,000 Words" CDRom (Scholastic)

Other Must-Have Classroom Materials for ELLs

alphabet books

counting books

math manipulatives

math games

word games, such as Boggle for Juniors and Boggle™, I Spy Word Scramble Game™, Secret Square™, Scattergories™

board games, such as Candyland™, Shoots and Ladders™, Monopoly™, Clue for Juniors™

books on tape or CD

Web Sites for ELL-Friendly Instruction

Bebop Books: Multicultural Books for Young Readers at www.bebopbooks.com

EverythingESL: The K–12 ESL Resource from Judy Haynes at www.everythingesl.net

Colorín Colorado: A Bilingual Site for Families and Educators of English Language Learners at www.colorincolorado.org

Webster's World of Cultural Democracy at www.wwcd.org

Chapter 4

BASICS OF TEACHING THE ENGLISH LANGUAGE LEARNER: WHERE TO BEGIN

As you read through these strategies and lessons, think about the factors that affect learning for ELLs, the stages of language proficiency, and the underlying best-practice strategies you can apply to your teaching to support all learners and make the environment especially friendly for ELLs (Chapters 1 to 3). This chapter is intended to help you understand what to expect of your ELLs, given their backgrounds and proficiency levels, and will provide appropriate adaptations and modifications to use in your lessons.

You will notice some repetition of lessons and vocabulary. This is deliberate. You do not have to teach a new lesson each time you teach. Repetition and review are important to language and vocabulary development. As ELLs build confidence through repeated practice, they are increasingly likely to become active learners in their second language.

Beginner

As described in Chapter 2, the beginner stage can last up to eight months (and in some cases, it can be longer). In the preproduction stage of language acquisition, learners receive language in preparation for speaking. At the beginning of this stage the student may be saying one or two words, and pointing or motioning for what he or she is trying to say. Be patient. This stage of language acquisition is challenging for both the student and teacher and may include behavior ranging from making silly motions to crawling under the table. This is really part of the adjustment that ELLs make during the silent period, as the child is beginning to store receptive vocabulary and adjust to the new surroundings.

Put Yourself in the Shoes of a Beginner ELL

Picture yourself in a situation where you cannot understand the language being spoken around you. You want to make friends and participate but your limited language proficiency makes you fearful. Helen Keller once commented that not being able to communicate is more difficult than not being able to see.

Language learning is best when it is contextual and unforced and that there are developmental challenges and advantages among beginner ELLs of different age groups. For instance, a kindergarten newcomer almost fits right into the program because the classroom and activities revolve around developmentally appropriate activities for adjusting to the school environment, language immersion, vocabulary development, dramatic play, and so on. In contrast, a third grader is thrust into an academically challenging classroom, in which students have already spent three to four years learning together, and have developed fluency in reading and writing. However, if the older student arrives with literacy in his or her first language, this can ease the transition into the EO classroom.

Mostly, the beginner stage is a time for teachers to help the student feel safe and comfortable and at least understood as far as basic needs go. The suggested strategies and lessons that follow draw on techniques an ESOL teacher would use with beginner students: singing songs, showing pictures, walking and pointing, total physical response (TPR) activities, reading books big and small, writing activities, drawing pictures, following-direction activities, and playing developmentally appropriate language-based games. Activities are reviewed and repeated as needed. Small-group or one-on-one instruction in or out of the classroom offers much relief for the newcomer. In this setting, there is less noise and fewer distractions, as well as the benefit of receiving targeted instruction and immediate feedback from someone focused on their EL learning.

CASE IN POINT:
Fitting in Socially and Academically

One year I worked with two ELLs who were sisters. One was a kindergartner; the other was a third grader. They arrived from Paraguay a couple of months after the year had begun. The kindergartner, Lourdes, was immediately embraced by her classmates who enjoyed introducing her to the new environment. She easily fit in and became the darling of the classroom.

On the other hand, her older sister, Esme, had a long period of adjustment. The third-grade classroom was not conducive to a beginning language learner. She appeared sad and confused. When I picked up the two sisters for pull-out instruction, Esme couldn't wait for her time with me, while Lourdes didn't want to leave the classroom. She was having too much fun. So for a while, I shortened my time with Lourdes and spent more time with Esme.

Esme, however, could read in her native Spanish and I was able to help her begin to transfer her literacy skills to English. In fact, by spring, Esme turned out to be more successful than her sister in gaining English language proficiency. Can you guess why? Esme's native literacy and previous academic experiences supported her in learning the same concepts and skills in English, while Lourdes became frustrated as the other kindergartners began to read and she was still acquiring English. It became increasingly difficult for her to keep up, and she now needed more academic support.

A well-organized, language-rich environment is what a teacher aims to set up every year before school begins. Posting your name and the names of the students on the door, leveling books, and setting up clearly labeled learning centers are all ways you might prepare for your incoming class. These same structures support ELLs throughout the year.

Following are some ways to specifically prepare for incoming beginner ELLs.

- Try to obtain any available school records (see Chapter 1).

- Find out if your ELLs have native language literacy. You may be able to use printed materials in the child's native language to support your teaching.

- Learn as much as you can about the child's culture and educational background, including how to correctly pronounce his or her name.

- Find out if anyone in the school or school district speaks the student's language.

- Gather as many picture books as you can, especially picture dictionaries and alphabet books. Try to obtain an interactive picture dictionary for a computer (see resource list, page 27).

CASE IN POINT:
The Importance of a Name

Nikolaus was a 6-year-old boy who emigrated with his family from Eastern Europe. He spoke very little English upon entering first grade in New York City. His teacher was having trouble saying his name, so she told the boy, "That's too hard to pronounce! I'm changing your name to Michael."

The boy became known to everyone in school, including his future teachers, as Michael. Michael never forgot this experience and when he told it to me more than 60 years later, his voice was melancholy and conveyed a sense of loss. Michael was my father.

I'd like to think that things have changed in the many years since my father's name was taken from him, but unfortunately this lack of awareness around honoring children's names still occurs. I know of a child whose name continued to be mispronounced by school staff even after his parents clarified the correct pronunciation.

While some children may be comfortable with a name change and even embrace it because they want to be accepted, other children struggle with adjusting to our culture, and the loss of their names only makes it more difficult. Think about the message of acceptance we can send as teachers by simply learning the correct pronunciation of a child's name.

- Get a tape recorder with headphones. Gather a collection of books with low-level, high-interest texts on tape. Recorded books in the student's native language are helpful, too.

- Put together packages of school supplies for use in school and to send home. This is a great way to welcome a newcomer and make the transition less stressful for the whole family.

- Fill a basket with drawing, writing, and manipulative materials for the student to use when he or she has completed an activity or is waiting for your assistance. Include a writing journal too, if one is used in the classroom.

- Fill a basket with picture-based language games (see suggestions on page 27). These pictorial games can serve as icebreakers for another student or a small group of students to play with the newcomer.

- Create a basket of low-level, high-interest picture books in English. When you or a student has time to read with the ELL, it helps to have this basket handy. This basket can contain some books in the ELL's language too. (See the book recommendations in Chapter 5.)

- Put together a packet of low-level, high-interest picture books in English that can go home with the student. Include some in the student's language, if possible. Send home two or three books at a time.

- Have student helpers take turns guiding the new student. Make sure the "shifts" aren't too long (perhaps one for each subject area).

- Check to find the closest local ESOL program for adults and other community services and encourage the child's parents to attend these programs. Frequently district or local community colleges offer a program.

- Prepare yourself. There is an adjustment period for you, the class, and your ELL student. In the classroom, if the student is totally inundated with English, the situation will be stressful. You may have a range of feelings from helpless to frustrated, but it's important to maintain your typical classroom decorum.

STRATEGY: HELP THE STUDENT FEEL SAFE AND COMFORTABLE

Yes, we strive to do this for all students, but it is especially important to communicate this to our ELLs. Following are some suggestions that will ease the transition into the classroom.

- Introduce the newcomer to each of his or her classmates several times. An ELL is not only putting names to faces, but processing new sounds with each name.

- Use short phrases, speak in a natural way, and speak at a slower pace.

- Take the student around your classroom, pointing to and naming various areas, tools, and so on. Be sure to seat the child close to you or a friendly student.

- Take the student on a tour of the school, pointing out bathrooms, the nurse's office, main office, cafeteria, and so on. Children learn how to say "bathroom" and "water" very quickly!

- Assign students to be "guides" and "buddies" for the newcomer. They can repeat these tours as needed, and sit with the newcomer to work on activities or play games.

- Provide many visual aids, including pictorial representations of commonly used words and phrases and of feelings (e.g., faces showing emotions), so you and your students have a reference to point to.

- Provide access to math manipulative materials so math concepts can be clearly demonstrated to and by the student.

- Review and name the parts of your daily classroom routine so the student can begin to know what to expect.

- Make sure the student has food, a snack, and proper clothing for outdoor play to ease his or her transition. I have often "borrowed" an extra jacket from the lost-and-found. Class parents can also be helpful in finding extra outerwear. Naming the food, time of day, and proper clothing items helps build vocabulary.

- Try to incorporate the techniques of TPR into your directions or teaching, as demonstrated in the following lesson.

First Lessons

For the newcomer, adjustments to the new classroom environment are the first lessons in understanding the new culture and language. Any sort of communication, like indicating that it's snack time or showing how to ask to go to the bathroom, is part of language learning and building vocabulary. These language basics will need to be repeated day after day until the newcomer's comfort level and understanding is apparent by his or her correct behavior and facial expressions.

Following are some lesson ideas for applying the strategy points listed above to help ELLs adjust to their environment.

- Provide a writing journal and have the student write reflections in his or her native language, if possible. Encourage her or him to draw pictures to go along with what is written. Use pictorial representations of school, home, sports games, and so on to provide possible topics. You or a classmate can respond to the ELL in the journal by drawing a picture and writing some related words in English. If the ELL is not literate in his or her first language, write one English word at a time and draw a pictorial representation of it, inviting the ELL to respond with a drawing.

- Show the student how to use the tape player, the computer, and other classroom materials. Place a red sticker on the stop button, a green sticker on the play button and a yellow sticker on the rewind button of the tape deck. Demonstrate how the buttons work. Show the student a variety of books on tape, including fiction and nonfiction, and have him or her draw a picture about what he or she has listened to in a journal.

- Provide as much visual support as possible. Primary classrooms tend to have many pictorial or rebus charts listing student names, daily activities, and names of centers. The variations here will depend on the age of the ELL and his or her first language literacy. (If there is time to prepare the class before the ELL's arrival, involve the whole class in making picture cards for *recess, bathroom, lunch, playground, happy, sad*, and so forth.) Check frequently for understanding. Your goal here is to keep the student in the loop as much as possible. Use the visual representations of facial expressions for you and the student to touch or hold up during a lesson.

■ Consider that students may have knowledge of the subjects you are teaching. *What the newcomer is able to demonstrate is only a very small part of what he or she knows.* Visual aids like maps, picture dictionaries and appropriate hands-on materials can help you tap into a student's knowledge. Math is a subject area in which many ELLs can be comfortable since numbers are the same across most cultures. It's an incredible experience to see an ELL's eyes light up at the sight of something familiar during a lesson.

Mid-Beginner

ELLs at this stage are just beginning to use simple words and phrases to speak with you and their peers. They need to have plenty of time to interact informally in order to practice common phrases to get along socially and follow routines.

Out on the playground during recess, you might hear a mid-beginner ELL speaking more English than he or she does in class. Social situations are far less demanding than the classroom, and learning in this setting often comes more naturally because the language is contextualized. Recess provides a place where the newcomer gets a break from listening to academic English or, if other children who speak his or her language are present, a break from English altogether. You may want to share this information with school personnel who don't show a lot of empathy for these young children. Statements like, "You're in school now! We speak English here!" are not a good idea pedagogically and such comments interfere with the acculturation process.

At recess, take time to notice how quickly children learn to communicate with each other. They point, gently tap, demonstrate, model, use facial expressions, and seem to move their bodies in any way they can to communicate. Provide opportunities within the classroom for informal groupings and cooperative learning so that ELLs can interact more naturally with their peers.

Language Learning Takes Time

It takes the average second-language learner two years to acquire basic interpersonal communication skills (BICS). And it can take five to seven years to develop a grade-appropriate knowledge of academic language (cognitive academic language proficiency, or CALP).

At the end of this stage, you will begin to see the child make a breakthrough and experiment with using many more words and phrases. This is an exciting time for both the student and for you as it signals that all the learning that has been going on internally is finally emerging in a way that will help the child make much more progress with the support of you and his or her peers.

STRATEGY: TOTAL PHYSICAL RESPONSE (TPR)

Teaching children that it's okay to point and communicate with gestures may not feel right to you, and you may find that students from other cultures are reluctant to point because they've been taught that pointing is impolite. However, in the context of a lesson, especially in language learning, where vocabulary is developing, appropriate ways of physical communicating can be demonstrated and taught. Using gestures to communicate is also part of developing social language lessons.

In TPR lessons, "command language" is a basic starting point for connecting gestures and actions to meaningful language. Examples include *Sit down. Stand up. Open your book. Close your book. Touch. Come. Walk. Run. Tap. Go back. Clap your hands. Stomp your feet.* Command language is also classroom management language and helps your ELLs understand classroom rules better as they get used to following directions in English.

CASE IN POINT:
Raul Makes a Sudden Breakthrough With Spoken English

Raul came into first grade without knowing a word of English.

In January, the students were learning winter and cold weather concepts and related vocabulary. We were reading snow stories, penguin stories, snowman stories, and the like. After we read a story about a snowman, I brought out a pocket chart and snowman cut-outs. Eventually, the students would build their own paper snowmen. This was a hands-on TPR-style lesson, and the snowy winter helped us get into the spirit.

About 10 minutes into the lesson, Raul's face lit up. He could not contain himself. He began to name every piece of the snowman in sight, grabbing word cards, snowman hats, noses, and snowman body parts. The language was literally exploding from him.

I halfheartedly tried to calm Raul down, while the children and I could barely believe what we were hearing: Raul was speaking English, out loud—comprehending and enjoying it!

In a TPR lesson, teachers:

- Demonstrate each direction

- Use single words or short phrases

- Say the word, then demonstrate the command

- Show pictures of the desired behavior

Lesson: Head-to-Toe Vocabulary Building

Background

This lesson is a great icebreaker for newcomers and beginners, and provides meaning-ful concepts with simple vocabulary around which to organize instruction. *From Head to Toe* by Eric Carle is a book you are likely to see in a kindergarten or first-grade classroom. In this book, a child character interacts with various animals, including a gorilla, giraffe, flamingo, and a monkey. The question, "Can you do it?" and the answer, "I can do it," are written, pictured, and demonstrated by both the animals and the child. After the animals move certain body parts, the child character repeats the action. Various movements connect the reader to text.

Carle's book provides excellent visuals and leaves the ELL something to hold onto and come back to. This might be an interactive activity for a class of kindergartners or even first graders, in which the ELL is naturally included. Second or third grade ELLs might work with an EO partner to read and imitate the actions of the characters. Upper-grade teachers can apply the concepts by asking students to cut action pictures from magazines that mimic those in the book. You can glue these more sophisticated pictures on cards or the pages of a booklet of copy paper, and use them as visual cues to teach a similar lesson.

Goal

Students use the actions of the book's characters to learn some beginning English language vocabulary. Learning is reinforced by acting out the body's movements.

Objectives

1. The students will listen to the story.

2. The students will repeat the reader's words and actions as he or she reads and acts out the text.

3. The students will learn to point and to copy actions or gestures so they can "speak" with their bodies.

Procedure

1. Share the book with the children and let the pictures speak for themselves as you "walk them" through the book.

"I can clap my hands. Can you do it?"

2. Stop at each page, read the text, and demonstrate the action.

3. Point to the page; stress the phrase that tells the action ("bend your leg"). If you have a big book version, let students take turns touching and pointing to the pictures and words in the book.

4. As you read and talk, touch the picture of the leg. Point to your leg. Bend your leg.

5. Point to students' legs. Touch your leg again and bend it again. Repeat the commands verbally as well.

6. Point to students' legs again and encourage each child to say and demonstrate the action again. At this stage repetition is very important!

7. Repeat this process as you go through the book.

8. Repeat this lesson until the students become so familiar with the book that they can almost do the action before the page is turned.

Closing

From a seated position, stand and say, "Stand." Then raise your hands toward the students, indicating that they should stand. Then say "Sit" and sit, then indicate that the students should sit. Say and repeat the actions with students mimicking you. Then walk to the door and say "Go." Finally, wave goodbye and have the students copy the action. Many action words can be taught in this manner.

EXTENSIONS AND POSSIBLE APPLICATIONS AND FOLLOW-UP

Once the ELL understands that the lesson involves the demonstration and repetition of the actions, he or she begins to connect the words and phrases to their meanings. Then, more variations can be used and this type of lesson can be repeated, providing more opportunities for learning.

The following are variations of the lesson described above.

■ Extend the lesson to include common classroom commands, such as "get your pencil," "open the door," "get the paper," and "clean up."

■ ELLs can create their own version of the book *From Head to Toe* and/or illustrate their own actions.

■ Use command language as the basis for a language experience chart. After a special class, such as art or physical education, your students can help you write on a chart about the actions they did in class, using words or pictures.

Command language for physical education class

Stand on the line.	Toss the ball.	Pass.
Go to the front.	Pass the ball.	Play.
Hold the ball.	Walk.	Stop!
Throw the ball.	Run.	Wait.

■ As a class, brainstorm lists of words related to various aspects of school and list them on a chart, or have students work in pairs using individual word-work notebooks. Inviting students to add simple illustrations can enable ELLs to work independently or with a partner as they progress through the beginner stage.

A fun game that will benefit ELLs and even challenge the cleverest EO is to come up with different ways of saying, "Go!" Or ask, "How many other one-word sentences are there?"

More Books With Compelling Visuals

Pretend You're a Cat by Jean Marzollo (Dial Books, 1990)

Who Hops by Katie Davis (Harcourt, 1998)

The Feel Good Book by Todd Parr (Little Brown and Co., 2002)

How Are You Peeling by Saxton Freymann and Joost Elffers (Scholastic, 1999)

Intermediate

In the intermediate stage of language acquisition, ELLs have gained confidence in speaking and asking questions. Their conversation is more comprehensible and many ELLs can keep up with basic classroom discussions and activities at the primary level. Contextualized learning continues to be important, as well as frequent checks for comprehension. While the intermediate ELL can read and write increasingly complex sentences, especially at the end of this stage, using abstract language and making inferences remains a challenge.

STRATEGY: MODEL LANGUAGE TO TEACH QUESTIONING IN CONTEXT

One goal of using English to achieve academically is being able to formulate questions. Children need to know the language of asking questions and to understand the difference between asking questions and making a statement. Modeling how to ask a question and listing words and phrases that begin questions provides scaffolding for all students and helps ELLs begin to develop a facility with interrogative sentences.

Lesson: Leading Questions

Background

Questioning activities are well-suited to a nonfiction study and encourage students to gather and retell information and draw inferences—key reading objectives. This lesson was implemented in a heterogeneous second-grade class in which the ELLs range from mid-beginner to advanced. (I delivered push-in support every day for 70 minutes.)

The class had been studying frogs as part of a science unit, and we had incorporated frogs into a study of fiction and nonfiction writing. Each student had chosen a nonfiction topic to explore. Their articles were almost complete and the class was working on revising.

When adapting this lesson for your class, make sure all students have a piece of writing to work on or make it a whole-class writing lesson by modeling the writing at the overhead or on chart paper, with students contributing as you write.

Goal

Students learn how to write a question for an effective lead.

Objectives

1. Students will write a lead for their nonfiction narrative.

2. Students will learn how to write a question.

3. Students will use a question to write the lead for their narrative.

4. Students will learn how to write variations of the same question.

Procedure

1. Explain to the class that today they will learn how to write an effective lead for nonfiction writing pieces.

2. Review some interesting facts the class has learned about the nonfiction topic of study. With the students' input, draft a short paragraph on a specific feature of the topic. If students are volunteering facts from a book, then help them rephrase the facts, writing the ideas in their own words. ("You can find frogs in many colors—from scarlet red to black—and sizes—from a kernel of corn to a pumpkin" may become "Frogs come in many colors and sizes.")

3. Model how to turn the topic sentence into an interesting question lead. First brainstorm with students a list of words and phrases that begin questions so that students have a reference guide. (In our lesson, students changed "Frogs come in many colors and sizes" to "Have you heard that frogs come in many colors and sizes?")

4. Invite students to rephrase this question in their own words, using different questioning words or phrases to begin the lead for the class paragraph.

5. Have students review their own paragraphs and generate some leads phrased as questions. One of our second graders' paragraphs looked like this:

> Did you know frogs come in different colors and sizes? Frogs that live in the rainforest can be as small as your fingertip. Frogs that live in New York can grow to be a foot long. Frogs don't just come in green and brown. They can be bright orange, bright blue and even red! But be careful! Those brightly colored frogs are poisonous.

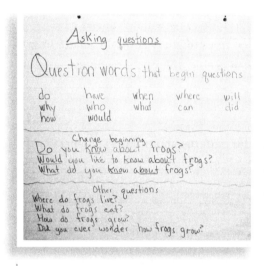

We began the lessons on a white board so that we could erase and change the language as the lesson developed. Later we transferred the information to chart paper for future use.

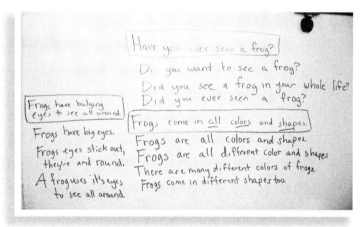

Closing

Students share their question leads with the class.

Follow-Up

Share and/or "publish" completed narratives as a class magazine.

Advanced

At the advanced level of proficiency, students are reading and writing with relative ease and understanding more of the academic language that is being spoken in the classroom. It is important to remember, again, not to assume complete comprehension. This stage can last from three to five years and as long as seven years for an ELL's language acquisition to be on par with those of his or her EO peers.

STRATEGY: TEACH WORD-STUDY SKILLS AND RECOGNIZE PATTERNS IN WORDS

Word study lessons give students the opportunity to play with words and language, learn about prefixes, suffixes, word families, and so on. Students engage in problem solving by looking for spelling patterns and tapping into pre-existing knowledge about language. Students hypothesize and predict and then test their theories. They can explore alternative ways of saying things. (It's something I love to do with students because they enjoy it so much!)

Lesson: Find a Pattern

Background

I recently taught this lesson with a heterogeneous third-grade class with advanced ELLs. Since the first week of school, students had participated in word study activities, including the creation of theme-based bulletin boards. The class was studying weather changes as part of a science unit.

Goal

Expand students' word knowledge through searching for patterns and problem solving.

Objectives

1. Students will recognize spelling patterns.

2. Students will use what they know about words to generate similar words.

3. Students will identify suffixes and apply them to other words.

4. Students will identify the parts of compound words and use them to form new words.

5. Students will use this lesson as a springboard to write a sentence describing their thinking about winter weather and then illustrate that sentence for the bulletin board.

Procedure

1. Write a sentence for word study that includes focus words. It can be a rhyming sentence or one related to a specific content area.

2. Underline focus words.

3. Read the sentence with the class.

4. Draw the class's attention to the words you have pulled out and underlined.

5. Challenge the class to notice something special about each word, such as the addition of a suffix, a doubled final consonant, a vowel pattern that rhymes with other words in the sentence, or a silent letter.

6. Have students generate a list of words that follow the same rule as the focus word. Add these words to the chart so that students can see how the rule applies and

so they can use the words later in their writing or transfer them to their own word study book. (The charts below show how different words can lend themselves to different kinds of word study.)

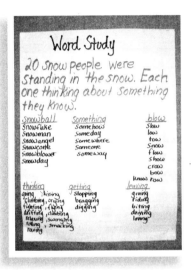

A winter word study of rhyming words, endings, and compound words

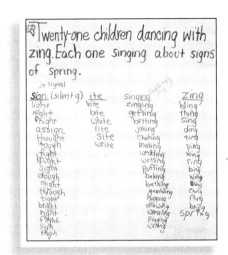

A spring word study with the *-ing* spelling pattern, silent *g*, and rhyming words

Closing

Students work on their own or in pairs to continue listing words and then sharing them.

Follow-Up and Extensions

- Students use the original word-study sentence as a springboard for writing a sentence about what they are thinking, which can be humorous or factual. These spin-off sentences can create a wonderful bulletin board, especially when illustrations are added.

- Students use their word-study words to rewrite the original sentence. In the example above, the sentence "Twenty snow people were standing in the snow. Each one thinking about something they know" might be changed to "Twenty snow angels were drifting in the snow, each one bragging about something they know."

Books for Word Study

Words Their Way: Word Study for Phonics, Vocabulary, and Spelling Instruction by Donald R. Bear, Marcia Invernizzi, Shane Templeton, and Francine Johnston (Pearson Prentice Hall, 2008)

Word Matters: Teaching Phonics and Spelling in the Reading/Writing Classroom by Gay Su Pinnell and Irene C. Fountas (Heinemann, 1998)

Teaching Phonics & Word Study in the Intermediate Grades: A Complete Sourcebook by Wiley Blevins (Scholastic, 2001)

Phonics They Use: Words for Reading and Writing and Systematic Sequential Phonics They Use (4th Edition) by Patricia M. Cunningham (Pearson Allyn & Bacon, 2004)

Chapter 5

BALANCED LITERACY AND ELLs

The components of balanced literacy are just right for all students. An ideal literacy-development program for ELLs in a mainstream classroom, balanced literacy supports both first- and second-language learners within the same class environment. Based on the research of Marie Clay (Reading Recovery) and Sylvia Ashton Warner (*Teacher*, Simon & Schuster, 1986), the program was initiated to help Maori children acculturate to the English-only New Zealand public school system and to provide a literacy instruction framework that would appropriately support all students. This chapter will look at how literacy-rich instructional strategies can include a sensitivity to language development for our ELLs.

Key Learnings From Balanced Literacy to Guide Reading and Writing Instruction

Balanced literacy offers various levels of support for students, from teacher directed to student driven, and immerses students in robust language use through listening, speaking, reading, and writing activities built around trade literature and other authentic resources. Students participate each day in a variety of different formats, including large group, small group, and individual instruction. They participate in guided and independent practice using reading and writing strategies. Skills are reinforced and vocabulary is developed during the literacy period through different instructional formats.

The program includes the following components: read-alouds, shared reading, guided reading with leveled books, and independent reading. (The specific benefits of each component are listed at right.)

Sensible Input for Beginners

Consider the difficulty of teaching a 6-month-old to say, "Daddy," by saying repeatedly, "Duh-a-dee." It's more likely that with natural parenting language (motherese) we say, nightly and often, "Here comes Daddy!" or "Daddy's home!" And that big smiling face comes into the picture with lots of happy sounds including, "Daddy's here!" "Look at Daddy!" Similarly, phonics instruction at the beginning stages of second-language proficiency would really be incomprehensible input!

Balanced Literacy Component	Provides Students Opportunities to
Read-Aloud The teacher leads a planned oral reading of a book or excerpt, usually related to a theme or topic of study. The read-aloud is usually read to the whole class.	■ Listen for enjoyment ■ Participate in reading for a purpose ■ Observe a fluent reader ■ Experience texts and ideas that are more complex than those that students can read independently ■ Develop listening skills ■ Increase and expand vocabulary and language use ■ Be introduced to texts that can be revisited in independent, shared, and guided reading
Shared Reading Building on the "bed-time story" approach, students gather in a small or large group to read and reread an engaging book in unison with the teacher, usually a big book/enlarged text.	■ Observe reading strategies in action ■ Have full group support ■ Participate orally ■ Read longer texts than in independent reading ■ Observe and practice reader-like behaviors
Guided Reading The teacher chooses a text for a small group of readers that has a common learning need such as level of fluency or understanding dialogue; the teacher reviews or introduces a skill or strategy and circulates around the group to monitor and assist each child as he or she whisper-reads aloud as independently as possible.	■ Benefit from teacher-controlled text selection based on reading level ■ Problem solve and practice strategies in a small group ■ Take risks with teacher guidance
Independent Reading Students read a book of their choice silently on their own.	■ Apply reading strategies independently ■ Develop fluency through rereading ■ Read with one-to-one teacher support ■ Self-select books ■ Develop reading endurance

Building Comprehension First

The components of balanced literacy listed on the previous page provide scaffolding to ensure that ELLs build comprehension and vocabulary. In this way, balanced literacy complements the methodology ESOL teachers use: a top-down approach to teaching reading that begins with comprehension as the goal and introduces the necessary strategies to help ELLs achieve this. So, rather than overwhelming ELLs with isolated sounds in a new language (phonics skills) first, a balanced literacy approach provides instruction and practice with pictorial, grammatical, syntactical, and semantic cues, as well as conventions of print. This context-rich instruction helps ELLs develop and acquire the vast receptive vocabulary and structural understanding that will support the rapid recall of the vocabulary they need to read.

CASE IN POINT:
"A Dandy Place"—Syntax to the Rescue

When reading *Freedom Crossing* by Margaret Goff Clark (Scholastic, 1980) with a group of advanced fifth-grade ELLs, I was surprised to find that these students, who were also studying the Civil War and slavery in social studies, were having so much difficulty answering a fairly simple comprehension question.

In the chapter we were reading, "The Slave Catchers Come," a young girl, Laura, and her brothers hide an escaped slave, Martin, under a trap door in their house. Slave catchers search the house, room by room, but they don't find Martin. The students had the opportunity to read the five-page chapter independently.

One of the questions in their comprehension activity, "Name the last place the slave catchers wanted to look for Martin in Laura's home," referred to the following paragraph: "Look in that closet over there," said another man. "That's a dandy place. Look good behind those clothes."

Although the answer, "the closet," required minimal inferring, and we reread the paragraph a second and third time, they were confused by the word *dandy* and they could not use it to help them connect *place* to *closet*. When one student asked, "What is a *dandy* anyway?" I realized their syntactical understanding was off.

Subsequently, we discussed the position of the word *dandy* as an adjective (syntax cue) for *place*. We talked about using the strategy of covering up or skipping an unfamiliar adjective in order to avoid getting stuck on it. In this case there were few context cues to help them figure out the meaning of *dandy* and though they could sound it out, their decoding skills clearly did not help them understand it either.

Of course, phonics skills are important and can be folded into instruction once ELLs have enough English vocabulary and experiences to apply them comprehensibly to words in print. We are ready to add targeted phonics instruction when ELLs are

- Not relying heavily on pictures

- Using more than one source of information (grammar, syntax, text features) to process text

- Reading for meaning

The same can be said for phonemic awareness. Certainly there is no harm in having a beginner ELL participate in these activities, but if you schedule a phonemic activity each day, this may be a good time to have your push-in support teacher work with the child on vocabulary-building activities. Or you may want to scaffold the phonemic awareness activity with a pictorial word bank.

Literacy Development and Language Acquisition

When considering a literacy program for ELLs we want to look at their needs as they pass through the levels of proficiency of language acquisition. While second-language acquisition is a developmental process, there are some interesting parallels between the levels of language acquisition and the stages of learning to read to consider. Using the chart on the next page you can compare these levels and stages. It is helpful to gain a better understanding of the time and needs to acquire language compared to the time and needs of children learning to read. For instance, a beginner ELL relies heavily on pictures to communicate just as an emergent reader relies heavily on pictures to understand and learn to read new words.

Academic language growth takes time. EO students have been developing their English language skills over the course of their preschool and early elementary years. So they are ready to develop academic language earlier than their ELL peers. Remembering to allow ELLs adequate time to develop both a second language and literacy is crucial to their success as academic learners. Here are some recommended literacy strategies for each language proficiency level, along with book recommendations to support your teaching with ELLs.

Non-Native Pronunciations

Non-native pronunciation of a word should not be considered an error as long as the student can access the meaning of the word. Their pronunciation will change over time as they read, write, speak, and listen to native speakers.

Language Proficiency Levels and Duration	Readers at Different Stages/Ages
Beginner (3 months to 3 years)	**Emergent Reader**
Low	(ages 2 to 7, preschool to grade 1)
Relies heavily on pictures and visuals	Uses mostly pictures for information
Says one or two words and occasionally understands written words and phrases	May recognize some printed words
Middle to High	**Beginning Reader**
Begins to understand more spoken language	(ages 2 to 7, preschool to grade 1)
Reads simple texts	Connects to their own experiences
Begins to connect first language to second language	Begins to respond to text
	Begins to connect own spoken language to print
Intermediate (1 to 5 years)	**Early Reader**
Uses short phrases and understands main ideas in context	(ages 5 to 7, kindergarten to grade 1)
Can retell a simple story	Becomes less dependent on pictures
Can read and write text that contains more complex vocabulary	Can retell a story
Developing and using more oral vocabulary	Can read familiar text and longer phrases fluently
	Is acquiring more sight words
Advanced (3 to 7 years)	**Transitional**
Reads, writes, and responds with an expanded vocabulary and has increased comprehension	(ages 5 to 8, kindergarten to grade 2)
Responds with longer sentences	Has developed a large core of frequently used vocabulary
Understands main ideas when reading	Relies less on pictures
	Has full control of strategies
	Reads fluently with phrasing
	Reads longer texts
	Can read independently
	Can map a story
Actively listens and can participate in group discussions	**Self Extending/Fluent**
Developing CALP (cognitive academic language proficiency)	(ages 6 to 9, grades 1 to 3)
Reads and writes materials and are within peer group level	Can read most words automatically
Can use language with relative ease	Responds to text comprehensibly
	Reads for meaning
	Can problem-solve independently
	Reads a variety of text

Multilevel

STRATEGY: KEEPING A READING RESPONSE NOTEBOOK

From beginner to advanced proficiency and emergent to fluent reader, encourage students to write short responses to each book they have read in an ongoing journal. A notebook can be used more regularly for individual work during independent reading, too.

Model each kind of response you want students to write before you send students off with their notebooks. (Responses can include lists, graphic organizers, and contextualized word work.) If a student is not ready to write then you can format the page and have the student draw an illustration. Show students who are ready how to format their entries with the date, the title of text, the author's name, and a label showing the balanced literacy component during which the response was written (for instance, you might use "S.R." for shared reading and "R.A." for read-aloud). This labeling will help keep track of students' growth and progress.

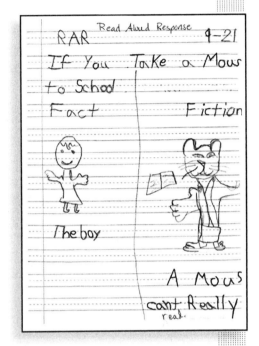

A labeled notebook page with different types of responses

Beginner

STRATEGY: SELECTING APPROPRIATE TEXTS

Selecting appropriate texts can be extremely important for encouraging and scaffolding ELLs in reading English. Even for an older ELL at a beginner level, starting off with low-level, high-interest texts that contain one word or one sentence on a page may be just right to help them build fluency. Remember that ELLs who are literate in their first language learn to read and often speak English at a faster pace than ELLs with no native literacy.

Have a variety of high-frequency texts available for all beginner ELLs. Make sure these books offer the following:

- Simple texts about common everyday occurrences that are heavily supported by the illustrations or photographs

- Concepts that are clear, appropriate, and support an ELL's communication in common social and school situations

- Concepts that tap an ELL's background knowledge

- A clear text structure; for narratives, a beginning, middle, and end; for nonfiction, clearly presented topic and details

- Illustrations or photographs that are bright and colorful and reflect a multicultural perspective

- Text that includes high-frequency words and is repetitive

- Writing that has a "guess what's happening" quality or can lead the reader to a conclusion or surprise

- A natural language pattern: for beginner ELLs, minimal semantic difficulty and syntactic complexity are important because they are processing so much language at once.

Leveling Books and ELLs

When choosing books for ELLs that have been leveled for guided reading, check out the online Leveling Resource Guide from Scholastic at http://content.scholastic.com/browse/article.jsp?id=4476, which provides equivalent Lexile and DRA levels for each Guided Reading level. For the ELL, the Guided Reading Levels are not enough—Lexile Levels and DRA levels take into account word frequency and sentence length (syntactic and semantic difficulty). Also, remember to preview the content: if the topic requires too much background knowledge, you will be spinning your wheels trying to explain it to a beginner or even an intermediate ELL.

STRATEGY: BOOK WALK AND TALK-AND-POINT

This strategy is appropriate for all beginning readers. The questioning, responding, and integrating of Total Physical Response techniques as described below and in Chapter 4, help ELLs acquire language rapidly and help you check for understanding.

Lesson: Connecting Pictures to Print

In this lesson the teacher demonstrates the connection between pictures and print by pointing to and naming pictures before and during reading.

Background

At the mid-beginner level students speak some English and are at the emergent stage of literacy. A book can be a friendly connection, a written smile. While emergent EO readers have more oral English language and receptive vocabulary than beginner ELLs, they still need heavy scaffolding to learn to read. For this reason, grouping emergent EO readers and beginner ELLs together in the primary grades works to everyone's advantage. The EO students serve as excellent models for speaking English.

Materials

A short, emergent reader (no longer than 8 to 16 pages) with a repeating language pattern in big book form and as student texts. *Rosie's Walk* by Pat Hutchins (Aladdin, 1971), *Have You Seen My Cat?* by Eric Carle (Aladdin, 1997), and *I'm As Quick As a Cricket* by Audrey Wood (Children's Play, 1998) are all good choices for this lesson.

Goals

■ To help students begin to make connections between pictures and print

■ To help students understand that print carries meaning

Objectives

1. Students will repeat the teacher's actions.

2. Students will repeat the language of the book.

3. Students will point to words and pictures in the book.

4. Students will "read" the book in pairs.

Procedure

1. Show students the cover of the book. Point to and name different objects on the cover. Ask students to do the same with their own copy. This helps them become familiar with the content and anticipate words in the story.

2. Continue on your book walk, showing students how you open the book and look at the pictures. Be more demonstrative, or dramatic as needed depending on the students' show of understanding. You are relying on para lingual (expressive, nonverbal) movements as well.

3. Next, look through the book again, saying single words as you point to a key detail in the picture. Discussing the pictures helps the students to anticipate the words that will be written or sets the schema for the text. Give students the opportunity to point to and name items in the pictures too.

Tip!

You can follow steps 1 to 3 with a big book alone (no student copies) as a lesson for lower-level students before reading the book aloud to them.

4. Model reading the book aloud. Then have students repeat this reading aloud together or chorally with you guiding them.

5. Instruct students to whisper-read the book themselves as you go around the table from student to student making sure that each student is tracking properly. Help students by pointing to items in the pictures and naming the items. Depending on their level of proficiency, you may be able to ask ELLs about what they're reading and seeing on each page (e.g., "Show me the barn." "Where is Rosie now?" "Tell me what you see in the picture." "What do you think will happen next?")

6. Pair students to read to each other.

7. Read chorally again.

Closing

Show and tell the students about your favorite part of the story or favorite illustration.

Give each student a turn to repeat your action, sharing his or her own favorite part. A less-fluent speaker may just show the part. You may also guide students' responses by framing the sentence(s) for them (e.g., I like the _____.) Or ask about key details and point to each illustration as you ask (e.g., "Do you like the red barn or the hen?" indicating the barn and hen.)

FOLLOW-UP AND EXTENSIONS

- Repeat the same lesson more than once, until students have almost memorized the text. This modeling and repetition is a key to building vocabulary and fluency.

- Model and then provide individual graphic organizers for children to draw a sequence of events.

- Write a new version of the book with your students. Gather words and ideas for the writing by taking a walk around the playground or somewhere else in school and use the language experience method, writing on chart paper the students' narrative in their own words for them to read and return to in future lessons.

- Make sets of color-coded picture and word cards for matching activities, such as a small-group activity in which each student holding a picture card must find the student holding the word card that names his or her picture.

- Use highlighting tape to teach vocabulary or emphasize high-frequency words.

Intermediate

As ELLs develop a larger oral and written sight-word vocabulary, they are able to move into the early fluency stage of reading. It is important to select texts that the ELL can comfortably read and work with for the following lesson.

STRATEGY: USING A GRAPHIC ORGANIZER

Long used for helping children organize ideas and concepts into a meaningful, accessible visual representation, graphic organizers are an especially useful tool for intermediate ELLs, who can write their ideas as single words or short phrases and use the organizer as a scaffold to write longer pieces or participate in discussions. Of course, you will want to match the right type of organizer—sequential, hierarchical, cyclical, or conceptual—to your lesson. *Graphic Organizers: Visual Strategies for Active Learning* by Karen Bromley, Linda DeVitis, and Marcia Modlo (Scholastic, 1995) gives detailed explanations with examples of each type of organizer.

Lesson: Graphic Organizers for Retelling

In this lesson, the classroom teacher and I used a storyboard organizer shown on page 52, from *The Big Book of Reproducible Graphic Organizers* by Jennifer Jacobson and Dottie Raymer

Suggested Texts for Beginner ELLs (Emergent to Beginning Readers)

Just Like Daddy by Frank Asch (Simon and Schuster, 1987)

Making a Memory by Margaret Ballinger (Scholastic, 1996)

Brown Bear, Brown Bear, What Do You See? by Eric Carle (Henry Holt, 1992)

From Head to Toe by Eric Carle (Harper Collins, 1997)

Freight Train by Donald Crews (Greenwillow, 1992)

Who Is Tapping at My Window by A.G. Deming (Puffin, 1988)

The Everything Book by Denise Fleming (Henry Holt, 2000)

The Haircut by Susan Harleg and Shane Armstrong (Scholastic, 1996)

My Dog Talks by Gail Herman (Scholastic, 1995)

There Is a Town by Gail Herman (Random House, 1996)

Legs by Rachel Gosset and Margaret Ballinger (Scholastic, 1996)

What Do You Like? by Michael Grejniec (North-South, 1995)

Rain by Robert Kalan (Greenwillow Books, 1978)

I See You Saw by Nurit Karlin (Harper Trophy, 1997)

Kites by Bettina Ling (Scholastic, 1994)

Who Is Coming? by Pat McKissak (Regensteiner, 1986)

Jelly Beans for Sale by Bruce McMillan (Scholastic, 1996)

Go Away Dog by Joan L. Nodset (Harper Trophy, 1991)

My Messy Room by Mary Packard (Scholastic, 1993)

Turtle and Snake and the Christmas Tree by Kate Spohn (Puffin, 2001)

Have You Seen My Duckling? by Nancy Trafuri (Greenwillow, 1984)

The Three Little Pigs retold by Harriet Ziefert (Puffin/Penguin, 1995)

Leveled Readers and Series Books

All Aboard Reading books (Grosset and Dunlap)

Scholastic High Frequency Readers (Scholastic)

Bebop Books (Lee and Low) (Highly recommended for their multicultural content and appropriate leveling correlated to these assessment programs: DRA, EDL, and INT. Titles include *Laundry Day*, *My Family*, *Loose Tooth*, *Cold and Hot*, and *Carmen's Colors*.)

Clifford series by Norman Bridwell (Scholastic)

Biscuit series by Alyssa Stain Capucilli (Scholastic)

Spot series by Eric Hill (Puffin) (Available in Spanish and in big book format)

A Bug, a Boy and a Bear series by David McPhail (Scholastic)

My/Mi(s) bilingual series by Rebecca Emberly (Little Brown) (Titles include *My Clothes/Mi Ropa*, *My Animals/Mis Animals*, *My Numbers/Mis Numeros*, *My Food/Mi Comida*.)

STORY BOARD

Draw and write the events of the story on the story board. Record them in the correct order.

1. First Max and Kate were rolling out dough.

2.

3. Next Mommy puts the dough in the oven.

Then they spread tomato sauce and sprinkled dried cheese.

4. Finally Max and Kate have pizza.

5.

6.

Ab Schiffo-Danoff

Storyboards help ELLs sequence events with both word and picture cues.

(Scholastic, 1999). We enlarged the organizer to poster size for the class mini-lesson and prepared individual copies for students to use during their independent work.

We also had a story from *Ladybug* magazine enlarged to poster format so we could use it as a shared reading text. We chose other stories for independent work, according to students' different literacy levels.

Materials

Graphic organizer (enlarged copy and student copies), shared reading text, pencils

Goal

Students learn how to use a graphic organizer to retell a story incorporating the sequence of events.

Objectives

1. Students will listen to a story.

2. Students will help teacher retell the story including the sequence of events.

3. Students will read independently.

4. Students will use individual graphic organizers to write and retell the story they read including the sequence of events.

Procedure

1. With the class look at the cover and do a picture walk, discussing what they see in the pictures. Call on three students to make predictions about the story.

2. Read the story aloud without stopping.

3. Read aloud the story again and stop to discuss each key event (focus on three to five events).

4. Call on students to retell the story aloud, using the key events. Model how to fill out the graphic organizer poster with each key event they name.

5. Hand out student copies of the graphic organizer.

6. Instruct students to read their independent reading stories once all the way through, then reread the story, and fill in the graphic organizer.

7. If there is a student who cannot read, read a short text to them and have them draw picture responses in the graphic organizer.

Closing

Choose three students or more as time allows to use their graphic organizers to retell the story they read.

Pictured at right is a high-beginner's summary of *Mud Tortillas* by Barbara M. Flores (Bebop Books/Lee and Low). Students in this class had practiced this lesson a few times over a two month period, and at this point they were ready to write events in the story into paragraph form. During independent reading, the high-beginner read *Mud Tortillas* with me several times and then practiced reading it independently before responding (the book was just above his independent reading level, so he needed extra support). He wrote one page with some assistance. Meanwhile, more advanced students read their books, at an independent reading level, both independently and in a guided reading group and wrote two to four pages of a summary response independently. Differentiating the text levels and the reading support for these students helped them all to succeed.

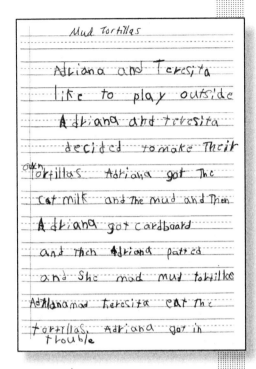

A high-beginner's summary response

FOLLOW-UP AND EXTENSIONS

▨ Have students use their graphic organizers to retell the story they read in sentence and paragraph form.

▨ Plan other opportunities for students to use the same graphic organizer.

▨ Use other graphic organizers.

▨ Use other graphic organizers to explore other types of writing, such as a sequential organizer for a procedural text (see Chapter 6).

Suggested Texts for High-Beginner to Intermediate ELLs (Early Fluency to Transitional Readers)

Chocolate Chip Hippo by Vincent Andriani (Scholastic, 1994)

Digby and Kate by Barbara Baker (EP Dutton, 1988)

The Case of the Cat's Meow by Crosby Bonsall (Harper Collins, 1965)

Arthur's Reading Race by Marc Brown (Random House, 1996)

Icy Watermelon by Mary Sue Galindo (Arte Publico, 2001)

Mrs Brice's Mice by Syd Hoff (Harper Collins, 1988)

Dragon Gets By by Dav Pilkey (Scholastic, 1991)

Outside Dog by Charlotte Pomerantz (Harper Trophy, 1993)

The Adventures of Snail by John Stadler (Harper Trophy, 1993)

Amanda Pig and Her Big Brother Oliver by Jean Van Leeuwen (Puffin, 1994)

Series Books

Young Cam Jansen series by David Adler (Viking)

Frog and Toad series by Arnold Lobel (Harper and Row) (Titles include *Frog and Toad All Year, Frog and Toad Are Friends, Frog and Toad Together, Days With Frog and Toad*)

Advanced ELLs

At this stage ELLs are ready to work on more challenging activities that support their growth as higher-level thinkers. Their cognitive academic language proficiency is growing stronger every day and they can apply their growing vocabulary and their reading and writing skills more effectively to develop and express their ideas. For example, they are able to grasp the underlying meaning of a text more readily and they can rephrase and paraphrase more complex ideas.

Below are strategies and accompanying lessons for a character study that helps readers build their "cognitive net" (the web of information a reader is able to capture and later recall about the stories or information he or she reads). By expanding this cognitive net, ELLs can more actively participate in higher-level questioning activities that involve inferring, predicting, questioning, and connecting to the characters—the subject of the lesson series below.

STRATEGIES: SCAFFOLDING MATERIALS AND TEACHING FORMATS

With some scaffolding, most advanced ELLs can keep up with their peers during higher-level thinking activities. You'll want to support them by:

- Having a range of books on a similar subject at different reading levels, so everyone can work on and discuss the same topics and share related vocabulary

- Providing a scaffolded sequence of teaching formats: move from shared reading instruction to guided reading or book groups

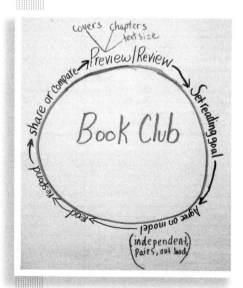

A cyclical organizer reminds book groups of the process for reading and responding together.

Lesson Series: Character Study and Response

All the lessons in this unit prepare students to respond thoughtfully to the set of character-based response questions on page 55. Each question was introduced and a response was modeled either through shared reading or read-aloud experiences. Each student was given a copy of the questions to keep in his or her reading notebook. (So that ELLs do not get stuck phrasing the beginning of their responses, the question set includes a sentence starter to scaffold students' answers.)

Materials

Books that reflect the reading levels of your students and that have strong central characters; character study questions.

Goals

Provide opportunities for using higher-level thinking skills and strategies based on literacy experiences.

Objectives

1. The students will read assigned text.

2. The students will respond to questions about the characters in the text.

Character Study Questions

Use the characters' names when responding to the questions.

1. What are you learning from one of the characters in the story? Give evidence from the text.
I am learning that . . .
One example from the story is . . .

2. Who is the most interesting character? Why?
The most interesting character is . . .
I think this because . . .

3. How do the characters feel about one another? How do you know?
The characters (use names) . . .
I can tell this because in the story . . .

4. Which character is the most believable? What makes him/her seem real? Or why does this character seem real to you?
The most believable character is . . .
He or she seems real to me because . . .

5. Which character is the fairest? Or use another character trait to discuss a character.
I think _____ is the fairest character because of the time . . .
      (character's name)

6. Did the character have choices? What were they? Describe the outcome.
One choice _____ had was to _____ or _____.
     (character's name)
When he/she made the choice this is what happened.

7. How has the character changed from the beginning of the story to this point in the story? Give evidence from the text.
_____ has changed since the beginning of the story. He/She . . .
(character's name)

8. Who is a character that plays a small role and why is he/she important?
_____ is a character that plays a small role. He/She is important because
(character's name)

9. What are the most important events that reveal the character?
One important event that tells me about _____ is . . .
      (character's name)
Another important event is when . . .
The next important event was when . . .

Easy Ways to Reach and Teach English Language Learners © 2008 by Valerie Schiffer-Danoff, Scholastic Teaching Resources page 55

3. The students will synthesize their responses to demonstrate understanding of character development.

Procedure

1. Choose about two to four books for modeling. You can use the same book more than once and touchstone back to it.

2. Tell the class that they will be learning about characters through a character study and invite students to identify favorite characters they have read about throughout the year.

3. Over the course of several weeks, use shared reading and read-alouds with the texts you've chosen to introduce and model a response for each question on the Character Study Questions page. On chart paper write the questions and a model response or sentence starter for students to refer to throughout the study. You may also want to photocopy the question page for students.

4. Form guided reading groups or books groups (or literature circles) organized around this study. The guided reading groups or book groups will be working on the same questions for responses that you've covered during your class modeling. Children will work on these responses independently too.

March 21, 2006
Thunder Cake
by Patricia Polacco

How has the character changed from the beginning of the story to this point in the stor? Patricia has changed since the beginning of the stor. She used to be afraid of the thunder storms. She would hide under the bed. Then her grandmother helped her forget by sending to collect eggs in the farm. She also walked through the Tangle weed woods jet tomatoes and strallberrys she also got milk from a Cow She also got chokalit and baked the thurder cake now she isn't sard any more. That's how she chaged from the beginning of the story and the End of the story.

I can describe a character. Toad is mean to the animals that hlp Toad find his button. Toad wanted Frog to woke hem up in May. toad gave Frog hes Jaket because pecus Toad gave Frog a hard time

Pictured at left is a response to *Thundercake* by Patricia Polacco (Putnam, 1997) written during read-aloud by an advanced ELL student who was at the transitional stage of reading. In the response to the story "A Lost Button" from *Frog and Toad Are Friends* by Arnold Lobel (Harper & Row, 1970) at right, modifications were made by the teacher to differentiate for this intermediate ELL.

Closing

Each lesson about responding to characters will have its own closing. Have children rejoin the large group to share responses they've made individually or with their book groups.

FOLLOW-UP AND EXTENSIONS

▪ Based on students' responses to question 9 on the Character Study Questions page, have each book group choose a character. The group members will collaboratively write and illustrate specific events. This work can take the form of a diorama or triarama, which groups can present as a culminating group project.

▪ A great way to end the study is to have a celebration in which students share their work.

Suggested Texts for Character Studies

Arthur's Mystery Envelope by Marc Brown (Little Brown, 1998)

Nasty Stinky Sneakers by Eve Bunting (Harper Trophy, 1995)

The Most Beautiful Place in the World by Ann Cameron (Yearling, 1993)

Verdi by Janell Cannon (Scholastic, 1997)

The Story of Ruby Bridges by Robert Coles (Scholastic, 1995)

How to Be Cool in Third Grade by Betsy Duffey (Puffin, 1999)

Nobody's Dog by Charlotte Graeber (Hyperion, 1998)

Say Hola, Sarah by Patricia Reilly Giff (Bantam Doubleday, 1995)

Russell Sprouts by Johanna Hurwitz (Harper Trophy, 2001)

Days With Frog and Toad by Arnold Lobel (Harper & Row, 1979)

Fox in Love by Edward Marshall (Penguin, 1982)

Get Ready for Gabi! A Crazy Mixed Up Spanglish Day by Marisa Montes (Scholastic, 2003)

Second Grade Ape by Daniel Pinkwater (Scholastic, 1998)

Bubushka's Doll by Patricia Polacco (Aladdin, 1995)

Thundercake by Patricia Polacco (Putnam Juvenille, 1997)

Mr. Putter and Tabby by Cynthia Rylant (Harcourt, 1997)

The Old Woman Who Named Things by Cynthia Rylant (Harcourt, 1999)

The Van Gogh Café by Cynthia Rylant (Scholastic, 1995)

The True Story of the Three Little Pigs by Jon Scieszka (Penguin, 1898)

The Day the Ants Got Mad by G. E. Stanley (Aladdin, 1996)

Grab Hands and Run by Frances Temple (Harper Trophy, 1995)

The Magnificent Mummy Maker by Elvira Woodruff (Scholastic, 1995)

ELLs With Native-Language Literacy

Lesson: Transferring Literacy Skills

Apply TPR and other strategies from previous lessons in this chapter to an independent or guided reading experience for a student who has native-language literacy.

Background

This lesson is designed for the mid- to high-beginner ELL who has native-language literacy and is able to transfer these literacy skills to English while also developing oral language through basic interpersonal communication skills (BICS). Using series books that have familiar characters and simple, natural dialogue helps the student both transfer reading skills from his or her first language, develop BICS, and build vocabulary.

In this lesson the student is reading "Tomorrow" from *Days With Frog and Toad* by Arnold Lobel. The student has read other Frog and Toad stories with the teacher before and is ready to begin to read on his own with teacher scaffolding. It is important for the teacher to check that the student is not just decoding but comprehends as well.

Materials

Student copy of a favorite series book at appropriate reading level

Goal

To further develop the transfer of literacy as well as BICS

Objectives

1. Student will take an independent book walk.

2. Student will make predictions about the story.

3. Student will read the story independently.

4. Student will read with the teacher and answer questions demonstrating comprehension.

Procedure

1. Have the student take a book walk through the story (see page 48).

2. Ask him or her to predict what the story is about.

3. Have the student begin to read the story independently. Check for understanding after a page or two. Then allow the student to continue.

4. After the student has read the story, discuss it in a conversational style that helps the student use his or her oral language to build background and context. (The script at right shows how this conversation might unfold.)

5. Ask that he or she read several pages of the story to you. Use TPR techniques and questioning to monitor the students' comprehension.

Script (reflecting steps 4 and 5 of the procedure)

Teacher: What day is today?

Student: Wednesday.

Teacher: Yes, you're right. What day will tomorrow be?

Student: Thursday.

Teacher: Yes, you're right again. Tell me something you will do today.

Student: Go to gym.

Teacher: You like gym a lot. Tell me something you want to do tomorrow.

Student: Tomorrow we go music.

Teacher: You go to music tomorrow. Do you like to sing with Ms. R?

Student: I like to sing, not dance.

Teacher: I like to sing and dance. But I don't like to clean my house. Do you?

Student: I help my mother.

Teacher: I wish I had a helper like you. In the story, does Toad want to clean today or tomorrow?

Student: Tomorrow, but Frog makes him clean.

Teacher: Do you think Frog is a nice friend or a mean friend?

Student: Nice and mean sometimes.

Teacher: Let's read and think about this question some more.

The student reads a couple of pages of the story aloud.

Student: "Toad said, 'Frog, your pants and jacket are lying on the floor.'"

Teacher: Point to your pants.

Student: (Points to pants.)

Teacher: Where is your jacket? Is it lying on the floor, like Frog's?

Student: No. In my cubby.

Teacher: You keep your jacket in the right place like Toad does. Let's read on.

As the student reads on, the teacher asks the student to demonstrate each activity or concept, e.g., *under, scrub, dust, watering*. Since the student has already read the whole story, this type of activity is contextualized. There are opportunities to elicit student output, check comprehension, confirm and clarify, and rephrase. It moves very quickly and is not done for the whole story so as not to labor the time.

FOLLOW-UP AND EXTENSIONS

- Have the student retell the story using a graphic organizer.

- Ask simple questions about the character or about other literary elements.

- Encourage him or her to read more books in the series to build comfort and familiarity with the characters, text features, and writing style.

Chapter 6

READING AND WRITING IN THE CONTENT AREAS

Reading and writing in content areas provides opportunities for summarizing, paraphrasing, expanding and experimenting with new vocabulary, and understanding more complex ideas. Content-area literacy work can reach students at different levels of reading and language proficiency, as long as students have access to a variety of multilevel texts. Additionally, a content-area study can be a rich source of vocabulary development for ELLs and all students as they interact with one another, sharing information about topics of interest, and create partnerships in learning.

Two examples of how to use nonfiction texts inclusively during your content-area lessons are presented in this chapter. The first is a series of lessons that build skills and strategies as students learn about nonfiction text features and apply their research on a specific topic to complete a poster project. The second example includes tips for using procedural texts to target a key writing objective (the informative narrative form) while integrating content-area learning.

Effective teaching strategies introduced in previous chapters apply to your content-area instruction as well. These include:

- Considering the essential vocabulary a student needs to know to read a given text. Highlight or create a glossary for your ELLs as needed. Focus on important words that appear in bold print, headings, and other nonfiction text features.

- Modeling a strategy or procedure before sending students off to try it in groups or independently

- Using graphic organizers, such as a K-W-L or Venn diagram, to activate prior knowledge and build background knowledge

- Introducing realia (real objects), maps, and other visuals like photographs and illustrations related to a topic you're discussing or reading about. The visuals will become images to which the ELL can connect words and concepts. You may find it helpful to use this strategy when introducing each passage of the science or social studies text you use.

- Providing a range of texts at different reading levels on the same topic to expose all learners to the same vocabulary. While ELLs may not retain all the language from their readings, they will retain some textual and visual memory, especially if the reading is scaffolded and contextualized.

- Teaching and incorporate study skills, such as reading timelines, maps, and flow charts; researching; graphing; and charting.

- Providing opportunities to develop higher-level thinking skills like predicting, categorizing, classifying, summarizing, comparing, and analyzing.

- Providing opportunities for students to work in pairs or cooperative groups to facilitate peer-supported learning and oral language development.

Unlocking Nonfiction Texts

The series of lessons below begin with the introduction of the SQ4R reading strategy, a six-step process that enables students to gather information before reading and set their own schema (framework of reference) for reading. The SQ4R steps include:

Survey: Preview the text by examining text features, including titles, subtitles, charts, illustrations, and photographs.

Question: Write or ask questions based on the survey preview to activate critical thinking and focus the reader's attention while reading.

Read: Read the text to answer the questions and begin to learn the material.

Recite: Answer the questions aloud with a group or study partner, checking for understanding. Long term memory is activated by speaking and listening.

Record: Write down the answers to the questions. Formulating the answers as written responses further reinforces learning and provides students with review notes.

Review or Reread: Review the answers and/or reread the text for more information. Here the student practices retrieving information and becomes aware of gaps in information that he or she will seek to fill.

Once students have practiced the SQ4R process a few times, they can move through the six steps efficiently and independently. This process works very well for ELLs, who benefit from using language in a variety of ways (reading, listening, speaking, and writing) to comprehend new information in English.

Nonfiction Study Lesson Series

Over the last three years I've team-taught second, third, and fifth grade classes with ELLs and worked on nonfiction units at each grade level. The series of lessons that follow are based on my work using SQ4R with the collaborating teachers in their heterogeneous classes. The lessons begin with using the SQ4R strategy described above to help students begin research on a self-selected nonfiction topic, continues with setting up journals to collect information on that topic, and concludes with using the information gathered along with an understanding of text features to create posters.

A student shares information she's learned about ocelots and the text features she used to create her poster.

The culminating poster is a meaningful way for all students to demonstrate their learning. Sharing their poster with the class gave students an opportunity to explain the concepts they had learned to a peer audience, demonstrating mastery of the information they had learned and honing their oral language skills, key goals for ELLs. (The rubric shown on page 65 shows fifth-grade expectations for a completed poster, which we modify for our ELL students, who may be able to include more illustrations, graphs, and other visuals and less explanatory text or who may need to write some of the text in their native language.)

You may want to dip into the lessons and teach one part or work with the series of lessons (plan to set aside four to six weeks).

Materials

Multilevel nonfiction texts (including trade books, encyclopedias, printed Internet articles, and so on), chart paper, student journals, rubric (see example on page 65), poster board, markers, rulers, colored pencils, colored paper.

Background

The classroom teachers and I began this lesson series in the spring semester, when students were comfortable reading and writing fiction and nonfiction pieces and could distinguish the genres. Throughout this unit, we included both group and individual projects to allow for a range of differentiated learning opportunities. For group activities, we formed heterogeneous cooperative groups and made modifications for our beginner to intermediate ELLS—including using low-level textbooks, writing frames, and translated materials, and having ELLs work on the illustrations more and write less than their EO peers. In this way ELLs could participate as fully as possible.

Goals

- Focus students on nonfiction by activating prior knowledge and building new knowledge.

- Provide opportunities for students to develop strategies for reading and learning in the content area.

Objectives

1. Students will learn and use the SQ4R process.

2. Students will repeat the process using different texts until they have gathered enough information to complete a poster for the final project.

Procedure for SQ4R

Part 1

1. Assign or let students form cooperative groups based on common interests related to a major theme or topic for which you have multiple nonfiction books and other texts at a variety of levels. Let the groups gather enough books so that there is at least one book per student.

2. Gather the class together for a mini-lesson and introduce the SQ4R strategy by writing "SQ4R" vertically on a chart and telling what each letter stands for: Survey, Question, Read, Recite, Record, Review.

3. Demonstrate, using a big book if possible, how to survey the text by looking at the cover, table of contents, index, graphs, pictures, captions, and any other nonfiction text features that are notable. Read a few title names from chapters, index entries, captions, and so on.

4. Have the class repeat the same process in their cooperative groups using the books they've chosen.

5. Gather the class again and discuss with students what elements they used to survey their nonfiction books.

Part 2

6. Refer back to your touchstone text to continue modeling the SQ4R process. Call on students to ask questions about this text based on their survey in step 3. Write the questions on a piece of chart paper.

7. Instruct students to return to their cooperative groups to gather and write three to five questions about their group topic based on their survey.

Part 3

8. Gather the class again and return to your touchstone text. Read it with the class and call on children to "recite" answers to the questions (give their answers aloud), based on the information they've gleaned from reading. Record the answers below each question on the chart paper. Finally, have students review the answers to their questions, checking for understanding. Instruct your students to repeat this process in their groups. Remind them to respond to the list of questions they've generated from their set of books (step 6).

Making Student Research Manageable

To make the research more focused and manageable, assign groups subtopics of a larger class topic. For instance, third-grade teacher Marisa DeAngelis used a book about the Yanomami and the rainforest as her touchstone text during a culture study. The cooperative groups each worked on a different element of the rainforest culture: clothing, food, shelter, and so on.

Part 4

9. Revisit the review procedure (step 8). Show students how reviewing their answers can help determine whether more information is needed. To model gathering more information and adding to the answers you recorded in step 8, touchstone back to your model text. Let students help you find additional information from the touchstone text and record it on the chart paper, adding to your original answers.

10. When students agree that you've gathered enough information to answer your questions adequately, write the information you've gathered into paragraph form, inviting students to assist you as you organize your writing with topic and detail sentences. Then instruct groups to do the same.

You can stop here and have students repeat the SQ4R process on their own or again with a group, depending on their reading skills. Or you may continue teaching about nonfiction text features and research skills by providing students with the opportunity to transfer the content-area information they gather about a chosen topic to a different format—individual student journals. These journals can serve as assessment tools to track individual ELL needs and support their written language skills throughout the study.

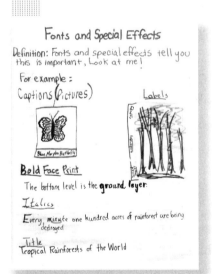

The model nonfiction text journal in our third-grade class included a "Fonts and Special Effects" page.

Procedure for Journals

1. Gather the class with their journals. Use the touchstone text to show students a title page. Discuss the elements and model how to set up the title page on a sheet of chart paper. Have students set up the first page in their journals as a title page, using the topic they are researching as their title.

2. Use the touchstone text to show students a table of contents. Explain or reiterate that this is a nonfiction text feature that shows readers how the subtopics of the book are organized and where to go to find the information. Make a model table of contents that you can fill in as you teach future lessons. Have students set up the second page of their journal in a similar fashion. (Students will create a page of the book after each subsequent lesson, and fill in the table of contents as they go.)

3. Using the touchstone text, point out one nonfiction text feature. Write the feature as a title on a new piece of chart paper and have students help you define and illustrate the feature on that page. For example, you might find a diagram in your touchstone text and make a journal page titled "Diagram." Your definition might be: *graphics that illustrate information so readers can picture what something looks like.* For your example, you might draw a diagram representing something about your touchstone topic. Then add the page "Diagrams" to your table of contents.

4. Have students repeat this process in their individual journals, using ideas and examples from their own texts. For example, if their topic is frogs, they might create a diagram of a tadpole or frog for their Diagrams page.

5. Teach a mini-lesson for each nonfiction text feature you wish to introduce or review, following steps 3 and 4.

Creating Posters

Creating a poster helps your students synthesize what they have learned about nonfiction text features and use the information they've read about their topic to create a final project.

1. Introduce students to the rubric you've created that outlines your expectations for the project (see the example below). Alternatively, create the rubric with students' input as you model how to make the poster (step 2).

2. Using the information the class has learned about text features and your touchstone text, model how to make a poster. Discuss possible layouts and how to incorporate graphics, photos and illustrations, titles, subtitles, and so on. ELLs in particular will benefit from the model you create. They can rely on both the written rubric and this visual example to help guide them.

Collaborative work on the posters reinforces content-area vocabulary and BICS.

3. Have students either work in collaborative groups or individually to create a nonfiction poster.

4. When students have completed their posters, invite them to present their work to the class. As a follow-up, encourage students to use the poster format to respond to other topics or for literature response.

Nonfiction Poster Rubric

Components	1	2	3	4
Text Features	Title Text Picture	Title Text Pictures (2 or more) Subtitle Sidebar	Title Text **2 or more of the following:** Sidebars Diagrams Pictures with captions Color or bold print Labels AND Organization is purposeful and clear. All spelling is correct.	**All elements in 3 plus at least one of each of the following:** Graph Map with map key/compass rose Diagram Cut away Photograph Drawing Glossary Bulleted points Pronunciation guide
Presentation	Some Color	Overall presentation is neat. All parts are organized and presented at an appropriate size. Color enhances the poster.	**All elements of 2 and** Text is edited. Lettering is clear. Use of color/design relates to subject.	**All elements in 3 and** Use of pictures is pertinent and valuable. Use of pictures supports the viewer's understanding. Placement of text features are appropriate.
Research	1 source	At least 2 sources	**At least 2 sources and** Research is relevant. Information is chosen carefully. Interesting facts are included.	**At least 3 sources** **All other elements of 3 and** Research provides viewer with full understanding of the topic.
Reflections	At least 1 reflection is answered.	Reflections have been answered. 2 are complete.	All reflections are answered completely.	All reflections are answered completely and are well written.

Procedural Texts: Content-Area Literacy Connection

A key writing objective for all of our elementary students is to be able to read and write simple procedural texts, also called "informative narratives" or "how-to" writing—and it is often tested on written assessments in grades 3 and 4. ELLs usually find the highly structured format and the clear, predictable sequence of steps in this type of text easy to access, which makes procedural texts a great teaching tool for building vocabulary and integrating writing in science and social studies.

Tips for teaching with procedural texts

■ Read aloud several short, authentic procedural pieces written for children, such as a simple no-bake recipe or directions for playing a board game. Have them identify helpful text features that organize the writing, such as an inviting introduction, a step-by-step description of the procedure, the use of time-order words to show sequence, and exact language to explain the steps precisely—how, where, and when.

■ Have students select a topic that they know "expertly" to explain to their classmates. (Some of my favorite examples of motivating topics students have chosen come from Lauren Cutler's second-grade class: making chocolate-dipped strawberries, caring for a pet, and roller skating.)

■ Use a sequential organizer to help students map their ideas; encourage ELLs to say each step to a partner before writing.

■ Provide a writing frame for ELLs, if needed, with sentence starting prompts, such as "Have you ever tried to _____? . . . The materials you'll need are . . .," and so on.

■ Provide time for students to read and demonstrate their procedure for peers.

■ Integrate with science and social studies by repeating the process with an activity, concept, or series of events—anything that can be easily demonstrated in steps, such as an experiment.

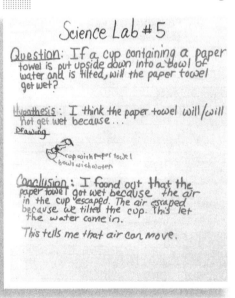

An experiment serves as a procedural text for science class.

Nonfiction Book Suggestions

For students:

Books by Gail Gibbons, Jim Arnosky, and Lois Ehlert

For teachers:

Nonfiction Matters by Stephanie Harvey (Stenhouse Publishers, 1998)

Nonfiction Craft Lessons by Joann Portalupi and Ralph Fletcher (Stenhouse, 2001)

Introducing Nonfiction Writing in the Early Grades by Jody Weichart Maloney (Scholastic, 2002)

Is That a Fact?: Teaching Nonfiction Writing: Grades K–3 by Tony Stead (Stenhouse, 2001)

Nonfiction Writing From the Inside Out by Laura Robb (Scholastic, 2004)

Chapter 7

INTEGRATING ELL STRATEGIES WITH WRITING

This chapter focuses on practices and strategies that encourage written expression and language development for ELLs. Included are suggestions for keeping journals, list writing, poetry, and revision. While these techniques can be adapted to any writing program, students benefit most from writing during a well-planned daily writing workshop. During this time, you can begin each session by teaching an objective-driven or need-specific mini-lesson, such as demonstrating elements of writing with models of good writing and teaching grade-appropriate writing targets, including writing conventions, revision strategies, and genre writing. A dedicated writing workshop time provides for large group, small group, and individual instruction and gives students ample time to grow as writers.

One key component of the writing workshop is a four-step writing process that provides a scaffold for independent writing. The steps are:

1. Prewriting: generating ideas for writing through activities that involve listening to read-alouds and class discussions, reading mentor texts, questioning or interviewing others who can share information about a writing topic, and brainstorming ideas. It is any activity you do before actually writing a draft.

2. Drafting: writing down ideas on a selected topic with an organizational focus

3. Revising and Editing: reviewing the writing independently, with peers, or with a teacher, to determine changes and improvements that will make the writing easier to read and more appealing to the intended audience. Sometimes revising and editing are treated as separate steps so that the teacher can teach mini-lessons on revising and editing separately.

4. Publishing: neatly copying and illustrating the final piece of writing to display it or share it aloud. Finished pieces often become part of the classroom library.

ELLs especially benefit from this process because it provides many opportunities to read, write, listen, and speak to and with their peers and teachers.

Journals: Authentic Records of Language Growth in Writing

Journals provide a place to record all writing—from personal thoughts to long-term narratives developed during the writing workshop. There are several types of journals to consider when planning for ELLs in your writing program:

❏ An individual log of all writing for the writing workshop

❏ A personal reflection journal

❏ A dialogue journal, in which the student writes and a teacher or peer responds (peer-response journals are often called "buddy journals")

All of these journal formats benefit ELLs in that they provide opportunities for students to write from their own experiences and get meaningful feedback from more-proficient writers.

Whatever type or types of journal you use, you'll find this a remarkable assessment tool: You'll watch the beginner ELL progress from writing one or two words to one or two sentences with the same sentence pattern. In the intermediate stage, an ELL will begin writing several simple sentences, containing minor grammatical errors and move toward writing full paragraphs that contain a broader vocabulary and more complex sentences. In an advanced stage of proficiency, the ELL will engage in writing fluent paragraphs that incorporate flexible word choices, sentence variety, and grade-level vocabulary. This is an exciting process to observe and support through regular feedback in the journal.

The following lesson begins in individual student journals used during writing workshop.

Lesson: Writing Lists

List writing is a very fast and effective way to get ideas going and begin the writing process. List writing is brainstorming all you know about a subject and quickly jotting it down in the same format as you might write a shopping list.

Materials

Writing journal

Background

It's important to begin using the writing process as early in the school year as possible so that students can use it with increasing independence during the rest of the year. One of the first mini-lessons I suggest—list writing—can also be used as a mid-year refresher to breathe new life into student's writing. This is a brainstorming technique for prewriting that often gives students enough ideas for writing topics to keep them going for months.

This lesson is appropriate for all students, including beginner ELLs, who may draw rather than write the list. You may need to provide some follow-up or individual instruction for the beginner ELL that shows how to create this kind of list in pictures. ELLs who have native language literacy can write in their first language.

Procedure

Part 1

1. From Arnold Lobel's *Frog and Toad Together*, read "The List," a story in which Toad writes "a list of things to do today," and crosses each thing off as he does it—until he loses the list.

2. Discuss the story focusing on the purpose of Toad's list.

3. On a chart, model the activity by writing a list of things you'll do today.

4. Have students write their own to-do list in their journals. Then let them share and compare items.

Part 2

1. Have students write another list titled "A list of things I can write a list about." They should list at least three or four topics they would enjoy writing about and sharing with peers.

2. To help students add more topics to their lists, have them pair up and trade ideas in a "Go-fish" type of dialogue: the first student shares a topic from his list and the second student checks to see if it's also on her list. If it isn't and it seems like an interesting topic to the second student, she may add the item to her list. Then it's the second student's turn to share. After a few turns, let students switch partners. (During this process, you may want to pair up with a beginner ELL or have a support person pair up with the student).

A conversation might go like this:

Student 1: Do you have "places I like to go"?

Student 2: No. I'll add that to my list. Do you have "favorite sports"?

3. Next, help students narrow their topics. Have them choose one of their favorite topics from their lists and write a list of subtopics (e.g., for "places I like to go," they might list a distant city, a favorite restaurant, the local mall, and so on).

4. Finally, from that list they can choose one of the items and do a two- or three-minute quick write (timed writing to generate ideas and build fluency). This piece can be expanded upon later.

As always, showing is the best way to explain what you expect. Recently, a couple of my high-intermediate students had difficulty understanding what "writing a list of things I can write a list about" meant. Making categories of things they could write about was a new concept and helping them to understand that they needed to choose broad categories required discussion and demonstration. Pictured at right is a student's list, which I helped her begin (she took over at "read a book"). She and I shared this list of lists with the other ELLs to reinforce students' understanding and with this model in mind, they went off to include more categories on their own lists.

FOLLOW-UP AND EXTENSIONS

■ Students share their quick-write piece.

■ Students continue the writing process with their quick-write piece or develop another idea from their list.

A list of writing topics provides high-interest material (the student's first choice is circled).

- Students develop a list that becomes a poem. For example, *Every Place I love to Go* or *My Favorite Fruits*.

- Students confer with you or their peers, asking and answering questions about their writing in order to expand upon the idea.

- Students use a five-senses organizer to revise their poem. This organizer has spaces labeled *see*, *touch*, *taste*, *smell*, and *hear*, in which students write at least one word describing how they associate this sense with their experience.

- Students choose one or more pieces to illustrate and publish.

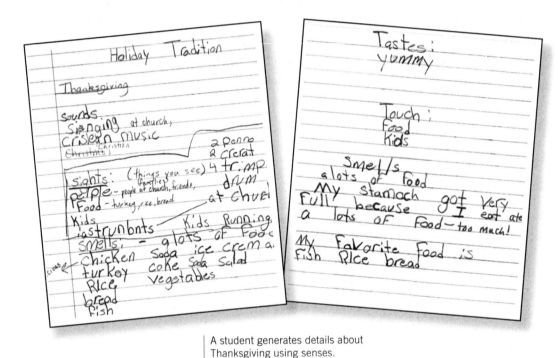

A student generates details about Thanksgiving using senses.

Poems: Engaging Entry to Written Self-Expression

Even students who think they won't like poetry can learn to love it. With kid-appealing topics and liltingly whimsical lines of master poets like Shel Silverstein, children's poetry offers models of fluent, well-phrased writing—especially useful for working with ELLs. Poetry is also a less threatening form of reading and writing than prose, and has fewer restrictive rules. This accessibility encourages Ells to practice reciting published poems and to take risks with self-expression in their own writing.

STRATEGIES

The next lesson on recognizing spoken and written rhyme and following directions requires a mix of strategies outlined in previous chapters, including brainstorming, activating background knowledge, modeling correct pronunciations, conducting choral reading, and repeating vocabulary in reading, writing, speaking, and listening.

Lesson: Directions to Draw a Monster

Materials

Directions for a Monster poem (see below), drawing paper, multicolored markers

Background

One year, collaborating teacher Marisa DeAngelis and I focused our poetry unit on literary elements such as mood, figurative language, onomatopoeia, alliteration, imagery, rhyme, simile, metaphor, and personification. We also covered format, repetition, and the author's intent. The class included mid- to high-beginner ELLs, intermediate and advanced ELLs, and a student with literacy in his native language.

When we developed this lesson, the children in this heterogeneous third grade class had been learning about poetry for a few weeks and were ready to explore rhyme. With our ELLs in mind, we sought a poem with a meaningful context and chose one that would show the students how to do something. Students' responses to the reading (creating a drawing) would support the development of their skills in following directions and listening, other important goals we had set for the class.

Goals

Children listen to a poem, follow directions, draw a monster to learn about the poetic element of rhyme and consider author's intent.

Objectives

1. Students will recognize rhyming words.

2. Students will listen to a poem and follow directions.

3. Students will discuss author's intent in the poem "Directions to Draw a Monster."

Directions to Draw a Monster

"First things first," my friend said,
To draw a monster start with his head.

This is a monster that soars and flies,
So to see he needs plenty of eyes.

Of course your monster breathes and blows,
Go ahead, and draw a nose.

If he goes north or if he goes south,
He likes to eat, so draw a mouth.

Too many to count above and beneath
This monster has a lot of teeth.

Below his cheeks and chin, please check:
Then be careful and draw a neck.

Our monster has a great big body,
Make it colorful and polka dotty.

Monsters like to walk on the street,
So give it many funny feet.

It is true, without fail,
Every monster has at least one tail.

Look at your monster, is it scary?
To me it looks very cheery!

Procedure

1. Write the poem on chart paper. To highlight the rhyming words, cover the poem with sentence strips so that only the last word of each line shows or list the rhyming words on a separate piece of chart paper.

2. Prepare desks or tables with drawing paper and sets of crayons or markers in many bright colors.

3. Show the partly-covered poem or list of rhyming words to the class and ask them to tell you what they notice about the words they can see. Students will tell you that each pair of words has the same sound at the end, or rhyme. (Save the list of these words on the chart for a follow-up word study lesson.)

4. To help them focus on meaning, ask the class to consider what the hidden poem might be about, based on this list of rhyming words. (Responses have included a child with a cold or a clown.)

Third graders display their monsters and make monster faces—the drawings all have the elements listed in "Directions to Draw a Monster," but each has a unique expression.

5. Then tell students to listen carefully as you read the poem because the poem will give them directions to draw something.

6. Reveal the paired lines of the poem one at a time and read the lines aloud. Pause long enough after each couplet to give students time to make a quick sketch and then switch markers for a variety of colors. Use this as a teachable moment to explain any words or phrases that may be unfamiliar to ELLs.

7. After you've read the poem, ask the children which body part the poem suggests, but does not tell you to draw. Give them a hint that it has to do with a special ability the monster has and invite students to reread the poem aloud with you. Students will tell you that the monster needs wings to "soar and fly."

FOLLOW-UP AND EXTENSIONS

■ Use the rhyming words from the text to teach a word-study lesson about common rhyming words that end with the same spelling pattern, or rime (*–eck* in *neck* and *check*), and words that rhyme but do not have the same spelling pattern (*teeth* and *beneath* or *head* and *said*). Compare all the rhyming words in the poem to see which have a common rime. Children can then use the words to list more words that rhyme and share rimes. Recognizing these spelling patterns can help children learn to pronounce unfamiliar words too.

■ Teach children about alliteration and have them apply the concept to naming their monsters (e.g., Monster Mike, Olga Ogre, and so on).

■ Present the drawings on a bulletin board with the poem.

■ Write other versions of the poem like, "How to build a snowman."

Revision is one of the most challenging parts of the process to teach, but it helps students focus their topics, clarify language, and elaborate their ideas. Practicing revising with poems can be a very flexible, simple way to introduce making changes to one's writing, especially for ELLs. This lesson can be adapted to paragraph-writing, as well.

Lesson: Revising a poem

Experimenting with the order of phrases in short, meaningful poems that they've written, children learn to understand the importance of each line in the poem.

Background

When working with second and third graders on poetry, we often begin with poems written by Jack Prelutsky, Shel Silverstein, and Douglas Florian. These include Shel Silverstein's poem "Lazy Jane," which only has one word on each line, and Doug Florian's shape poem about a sawfish. These poems are visually and linguistically accessible for all students, and especially ELLs. The poems students create lend themselves to the simple revision lesson that follows.

This lesson was very helpful to the students because the process encouraged students to work flexibly with language. We promised a celebration at the end of the unit, a publishing party, to make the process even more rewarding. Since second and third graders had completed the unit around the same time, we had a cross-grade-level celebration which included poetry reading and sharing in small groups.

Materials

Sentence strips, scissors, blank books, construction paper

Goal

Children learn about the use of lines in poetry writing.

Objectives

1. Children will write original poems on sentence strips line by line.

2. Children will rearrange sentence strips to reorder the lines of their poems.

3. Children will recognize that changing the arrangement of lines changes the poem's meaning.

Procedure

1. Model writing an original poem on sentence strips. (You may want to choose a topic for which you've done a class brainstorm. Then group the words into phrases on sentence strips. A four-line poem may be fine for the primary grades, while six or more lines are appropriate for the upper grades.)

2. Invite volunteers to help you rearrange the sentence strips to write the poem differently.

3. Read the poem through after each arrangement. Discuss how the different line arrangements change the meaning and sound of the poem.

Using sentence strips, children experiment with reordering the lines of their poems.

4. For students with higher levels of language proficiency, include other revision techniques in this lesson, such as checking for extra unneeded words or unwanted repetition, changing ordinary words to more exciting words, and rebreaking lines for effect.

FOLLOW-UP AND EXTENSIONS

■ Students cut up the sentence strips word by word then rearrange the words to write a new poem.

■ Conduct a lesson in which you add more descriptive language by writing new words on parts of sentence strips. Show students how to cut apart the original lines and insert the new words.

■ After students have written three to ten poems they can publish their writing in poetry booklets. For example, primary students might publish three poems in a trifold book.

Books for Teachers

Poetry Place Anthology by Rosemary Alexander (Scholastic, 1999)

Craft Lessons: Teaching Writing K–8 by Ralph Fletcher and Joann Portalupi (Stenhouse, 1998, 2007)

The Revision Toolbox by Georgia Heard (Heinemann, 2002)

101 Thematic Poems for Emergent Readers by Mary Sullivan (Scholastic, 1999)

Stepping Sideways Into Poetry Writing: Practical Lessons by Kathryn Winograd (Scholastic, 2005)

Books for Teacher and Student

Echoes for the Eye, Poems to Celebrate Patterns in Nature by Barbara Juster Esbensen (Harper Collins, 1996)

Bing, Bang, Boing by Douglas Florian (Harcourt, 1994)

In the Swim by Douglas Florian (Voyager, 2001)

What's on the Menu selected by Bobby S. Goldstein (Puffin Books, 1992)

Surprises Poems selected by Lee Bennet Hopkins (Harper Trophy, 1984) and other books compiled or written by Lee Bennet Hopkins

The Sweet and Sour Animal Book by Langston Hughes (Oxford University Press, 1994)

You Be Good and I'll Be Night by Eve Merriam (Mulberry Books, 1988)

A Pizza the Size of the Sun by Jack Prelutsky (Greenwillow Books, 1996) and other Prelutsky titles

Falling Up by Shel Silverstein (HarperCollins, 2003)

Did You See What I Saw?: Poems About School by Kay Winters (Penguin, 1996)

Bare Books from www.barebooks.com

Chapter 8

TEAM TEACHING WITH THE ESOL TEACHER

Team teaching—two or more teachers working together with the same group of students—offers you and your students many opportunities for improving instruction and achievement, especially for ELLs. This collaboration involves working together, mentoring, sharing, observing, and exchanging best-practice ideas to meet the needs of target students—and support the rest of the class.

This chapter shows how you and your students can benefit from team teaching with the ESOL teacher, what needs to be in place in terms of logistics and attitudes, and how you can make the most of the experience.

Why Team Teach?

There are so many advantages to working with another teacher. Let's look at some of the benefits you can expect when collaborating with your ESOL teacher.

An ESOL teaching partner can help you and your students in the following ways:

- Suggest strategies specific to each lesson or unit.
- Break down the lesson to manageable parts.
- Bring in additional materials to activate prior knowledge.
- Provide needed visuals or a range of texts at different reading levels.
- Modify lessons or texts to meet specific language or reading needs.
- Create a glossary of high-use words for the topic or subject area.
- Highlight and review essential vocabulary and concepts.
- Support ELLs in small-group or one-on-one instruction.
- Help teach and demonstrate lessons and facilitate group work.
- Give you additional information about the abilities, skills, and interests of ELLs in your class whom she has taught before.

Together, you and the ESOL teacher can enhance instruction in the following ways:

- Provide a wider range of teaching/learning experiences for all your students and contribute to their success.
- Plan units that differentiate instruction for various learning styles.

- Increase the comprehensibility of lessons and opportunities for teacher-student and peer interactions.

- Support each other in experimenting with new material and discover new ways of teaching "the same old thing" to make it new again.

- Evaluate, synthesize, and compare lessons to determine successes and understand and improve upon failures.

CASE IN POINT:
A Growing Partnership

I was assigned to support a group of high-intermediate to advanced ELLs in a fifth-grade class. The teacher, Michelle, and I began with a few professional conversations and decided to adopt a pull-out model to support the ELLs in her class, since the classroom was small.

As the fall semester progressed, we had time to learn more about each other, including the children's and adult books we loved, and our shared philosophies. She told me more of her plans. I made some suggestions. Many times we tossed ideas back and forth and came up with a plan together. It was clearly a case of "two heads are better than one."

One day when I came to pick up the ELL group, Michelle was about 10 minutes behind. She apologized and continued teaching. When she paused at one point, I raised my hand. With a big smile on her face she called on me. I asked a question about a word she had used, to clarify its meaning for the ELL group.

Michelle threw the question to her class. No hands went up. So, she asked me what I thought it meant. I asked her to read the sentence from the text again. And right there, in front of her class, we tossed ideas back and forth, using context clues to determine the meaning of the word. Children began to raise their hands to add their ideas and expand the definition of the word.

From that point on, our teaching changed. We decided to take more time to look at lessons together and to try to keep the ELL group in the class longer. One day when Michelle was beginning to teach the lesson on a chart in front of the class, I nodded toward the white board asking if I could mirror her lesson, adding some visuals and other scaffolds as needed. All the students became more engaged, seeing the lesson unfold in words and images together.

For the remainder of the year our partnership kept evolving. Michelle loved Shakespeare and worked very hard with multimedia tools to present a unit about Shakespeare to the class in the spring. Working together, we enabled the whole class to participate through partner and cooperative group work. We learned to plan more and more of the instruction together and eventually, I stopped pulling the ELL students out.

Though my schedule the next year did not include her class, we both developed great team-teaching strategies to use with other teachers . . . and we developed a friendship that continues to this day.

What Needs to Be in Place

These are the basic elements you need to consider in order to make a partnership with an ESOL teacher work:

1. **Time for planning:** No matter what advice you read about team teaching, the common thread for success is establishing enough time to plan and planning on a regular basis. Without consistent planning time, people with the best intentions can neither appropriately develop their lessons nor stay connected to cultivate a successful partnership.

2. **Commitment:** If you can make the time, then set your intention to be committed to the teamwork. In all my co-teaching relationships, my partnering teachers and I commit to being creative, respectful, well-planned, and reflective. This means allowing each other to take risks, setting boundaries if necessary, bringing lots of ideas to share when planning, and continuously monitoring and adjusting our teaching in order to improve instruction for our students. We also recognize that sometimes we need to try something the other person's way. Showing our ability to work together and our respect for one another in front of the children is key as well.

3. **Avoiding the 3 Ds:** Dishonesty, disorganization, and distrust pose a tremendous threat to successful teams. One of the best things you can do is to speak up when you feel uncomfortable with how or what is being planned or taught. This can be hard, but it's necessary to maintain an honest relationship and one that's focused on student achievement. (And, keeping in mind that there is no one way of doing something, you can agree to try a lesson one way and then come back together, assess the outcome, and try it another way if need be.) Being organized with planning and teaching materials is also central to efficient planning and lesson delivery. Finally, creating an environment where you can both take risks to improve your instruction demonstrates to students that they can take risks to achieve and that supporting one another helps the whole team.

4. **Time for the partnership to grow:** A great relationship takes time to develop. Start with a plan for co-teaching that is manageable for both of you. The more you work together and follow the three reminders above, the more you will be able capitalize on your strengths and the more collaborative you will be able to make your teaching.

Taking the Risk

Committing to a working partnership with another person can be challenging, especially when your partner may seem very different than you. But you may be surprised at how well you can work off of someone else's very different strengths. In fact, you never know how a partnership will work out until you try it. Having an open mind and a good attitude are key.

Keep these pointers in mind when working with your new partner

■ Always consider suggestions. Trust that another teacher has some experience to offer that is different from yours and will give you a valuable perspective.

- Ask for help when you need it.

- Be honest. State your opinions and establish your boundaries, if you need to. This is your classroom, so you should have the final say.

- Be ready and organized when the ESOL teacher enters the room.

- Try something new—you have another person to support you and back you up.

- Invite the ESOL teacher to share in your planning. Start small, even with part of a lesson.

CASE IN POINT:
Establishing Boundaries and a Common Ground to Build an Unlikely Partnership

For two years I have worked with a teacher 30 years younger than I am—a self-described independent thinker and worker. Yet what we have accomplished together with our ELL and EO students has been very rewarding.

At the time that I met Marisa, she was 25, new to our school, and beginning her teaching career. Our partnership began with finding some common ground: during lunch and other breaks over the course of a three-day workshop at the beginning of the school year, we discovered that we agreed not only on teaching approaches—we had read many of the same professional books—but also on the best places to work out and shop. We continued this rapport through her first year.

In her second year of teaching third grade we began to form our partnership. Now that we had some common ground between us, we needed to set some expectations and boundaries so Marisa could feel comfortable and in control. Marisa made it clear that while she wanted to team teach, she needed to feel at all times that the classroom was hers. She wanted me to share in the teaching when I was in the room. Of course, I agreed with her, and appreciated her honesty and forthrightness.

With a clear sense of our roles, everything else went smoothly: Our rapport during our planning sessions supported the collaborative work we did in the classroom. Not only did we share materials, we thoroughly examined them, often laughing together, as we both tried to figure out what it was that we didn't like about how a strategy was presented and how we could make it more available to our students. We consulted other resources. Then we came up with a plan for teaching it together by modeling it, with a modicum of melodrama, in front of the class. More planning and lessons evolved into seamless team teaching.

The 30-year difference in our ages and the 16-year difference in our teaching experiences quickly dissipated into what has become one of the best teaching partnerships and friendships I've enjoyed.

Models of Team Teaching

Having been a classroom teacher for 13 years, I understand how difficult it can be to have someone else in your classroom. It takes time to get to know each other's styles. My experiences as an ESOL teacher have taught me to allow that learning to happen, rather than forcing a co-teaching approach to work. In fact, there are many different ways a partnership can work and there is no one model you must follow. You may also decide to change the model for different students or different subject areas.

Here are a few team-teaching models to consider:

- Planning and teaching the lesson together with both of you at the front of the room sharing the delivery of the lesson or splitting the delivery of the lesson.

- Planning two different lessons with the same content, breaking the larger group into two groups and rotating the students through a lesson with each teacher.

- Having the ESOL teacher serve as a consultant with whom you meet to discuss modifications needed for ELLs in your class.

- Having the ESOL teacher plan a few lessons with you to show you how to use modifications and integrate strategies that would make the subject more accessible to ELLs.

Marisa D'Angelis and I work together, demonstrating how to read a text and record text features.

- Planning lessons on your own, sharing the plans with the ESOL teacher, and then having the ESOL teacher work with a decentralized group within the classroom.

- Presenting the lesson to the whole class while the ESOL teacher paraphrases and modifies as needed, mirroring your lesson or presenting visuals to illustrate the content.

- Demonstrating a lesson together fishbowl-style and then pairing students so they can work on the new skill together.

- Reviewing material with one teacher working on basic review with a needs-based group, while the other brings students through a higher-level thinking activity.

The benefits of having another professional in the classroom are incomparable to any other teaching experience. To make the most of the team-teaching experience, it is important to stay committed to a consistent planning time that is open, reflective, and organized, as I've detailed in this chapter. There may be rough times, moments to reexamine, even disagreement, but the rewards are numerous. And remember always to have fun teaching with your partner because when collaboration works, it works personally and professionally!

Glossary

Acculturation—the process of acquiring a second culture while maintaining one's first culture.

Assimilation—the process of replacing one's first culture with the second culture.

BICS—Basic Interpersonal Communication Skills, a common measure of conversational or social language skills.

Brainstorming—a technique in which a group generates a large number of ideas to solve a problem or enhance learning.

CALP—Cognitive Academic Language Proficiency, a measure of formal language skills of listening, speaking, reading, and writing used for academic learning.

Comprehensible input—language that is used in ways that make it understandable to the learner. This may include repetition, paraphrasing, and acting out.

EFL—English as a Foreign Language, meaning students learning English in their native country.

ELL—English Language Learner

EO—English-Only speaker.

ESL—English as a Second Language

ESOL—English to Speakers of Other Languages.

L1, L2—L1 is a speaker's first language. L2 is the second language acquired.

Cognitive net—the web of information a reader is able to capture and later recall about the stories or information he or she reads.

Language experience approach—writing down the students' narrative in their own words for them to read (the writing should reflect the students' exact words, even inaccuracies in syntax and grammar).

Para lingual—nonverbal; conveyed through gesture and facial expression.

Picture or book walk—sharing the pictures in a book and discussing briefly what the students see; moving through page by page if it's a picture book or checking out the table of contents if it's a chapter book. This pre-reading activity helps students activate prior knowledge, learn new vocabulary in context, and prepare to read.

Push-in support—assistance in the classroom from a specialist, such as an ESOL teacher.

Quick write—short, timed writing assignment during which students write as much as they can about a given topic, quote, or story-starter idea. Done frequently, this practice helps students build writing fluency and endurance.

Realia—a method of display using real objects in a graphic organizer or when teaching about a subject.

Rebus—a format that uses pictures with or instead of words.

Semantic feature analysis—a method used to reinforce concepts and vocabulary. For instance, given a favorite Halloween category like "candy" one might list lollipops, candy corn, M&M's, and gummy bears. To draw distinctions between these candies a list of attributes must be generated (e.g., chocolate, chewy, crunchy, and colorful). The final step is to set up a chart or matrix and check off the characteristics of each type of candy.

Sheltered instruction—a class in which ELLs do not compete with EOs for instruction. The teacher uses physical activities, visual aids, linguistic modifications, and other methods to teach math, science, and history.

Silent period—a stage during which newcomers do not produce language, lasting as long as a year.

Submersion—a sink-or-swim approach to ELL instruction, in which ELLs are placed in regular classes and required to learn at the same level as their native-speaking peers.

TESOL—Teachers of English to Speakers of Other Languages (check out www.TESOL.org).

Touchstone—refers to a book, story, or a past learning experience that is used again, in a different way or as a springboard for new learning.

TPR—Total Physical Response. In this method of second language instruction, developed by James Asher, students respond to commands that require physical movement to help them internalize the new language.

Word bank—a list of words about a particular subject, such as spring, that is generated by the class as a prewriting activity. The words are written on a chart so that the class can refer to the list.